100

THINGS TO DO IN

SONOMA COUNTY

BEFORE YOU

DIE

100
THINGS TO DO IN
SONOMA COUNTY BEFORE YOU DIE

• •

YVONNE MICHIE HORN

REEDY PRESS

Library of Congress Control Number: 2020922407

ISBN: 9781681063133

Design by Jill Halpin

Photos by author unless otherwise noted.

Printed in the United States of America
21 22 23 24 25 5 4 3 2 1

DEDICATION

To all who call Sonoma County home,
and to those who come to visit.

Photo courtesy of Pixabay

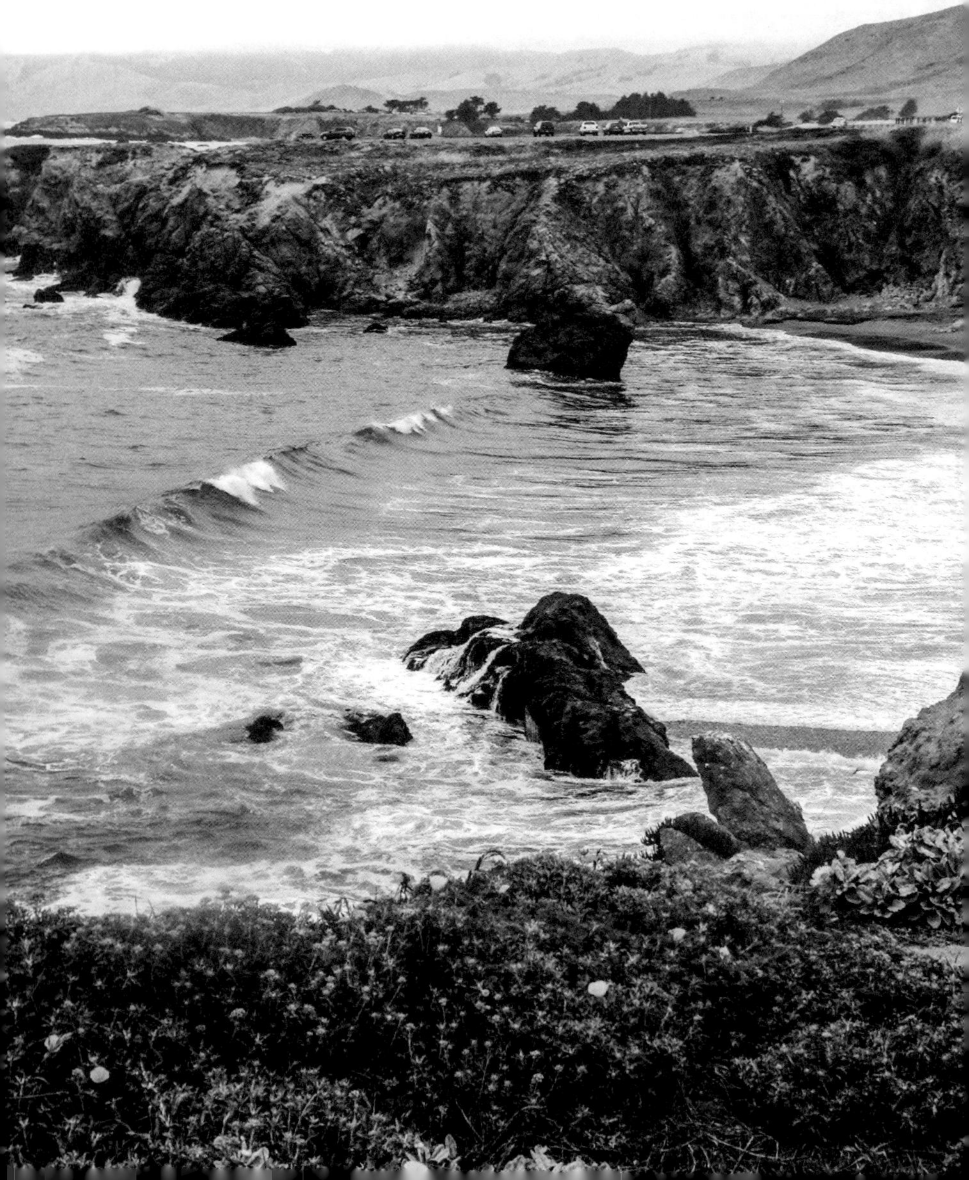

CONTENTS

● ●

Music and Entertainment

Sports and Recreation

• •

• •

Photo courtesy of Pixabay

Photo courtesy of Pixabay

PREFACE

What's a travel writer to do when a pandemic trims her travel wings? Enter Reedy Press with a gap in their best-selling *100 Things* series: Sonoma County, the place in the world I know and love best! I began my things-to-do list.

Without fail, no matter where in this wonderful world a writing assignment takes me, I return to where three generations of my family have called home with famed early 20th-century horticulturist Luther Burbank's quote about Sonoma County ringing in my ears: "the chosen spot of all this earth as far as Nature is concerned."

Mother Nature pulled out all the stops when she created Sonoma County's 1,768 square miles. She edged it with a spectacular, wave-dashed coastline; added in a winding river for morning fog to follow on its way to keep lush interior valleys cool; garnished its entirety with rugged mountain peaks and gentle oak-dotted hills; and blessed it with a climate in which everything and anything might thrive.

When I hear Sonoma County defined as "Wine Country," I take exception. Yes, it is that, but so much more—as you will discover as you turn the pages of *100 Things to Do in Sonoma County Before You Die*.

• •

FOOD AND DRINK

ROLL ALONG IN A PINZGAUER
ON A WINE-TASTING TOUR AT GUNDLACH BUNDSCHU

Step inside the tasting room of California's oldest family winery, and you'll see a poster that reads: "If you can't say, 'Gundlach Bundschu Gewürztraminer,' you shouldn't be driving." Good news: someone else will be at the wheel of the Pinzgauer, the six-wheeled, 12-person, Austrian military vehicle ready to take you on an off-road Rhinefarm adventure.

Since 1858, six generations of Bundschus have farmed the 320-acre Rhinefarm. Expect "Gun-Bun" tales, often outrageous, to be told along the way. At five super-scenic spots, selected estate wines are poured for tasting while you take in the views and learn firsthand how the wine in your glass came about. Midway, hop out to enjoy cheese and charcuterie paired with your sipping as you stroll among the vines.

2000 Denmark St., 95476
(707) 938-5277, gunbun.com

GO WILD OVER BAKED GOODS
AT WILD FLOUR BREAD

In tiny Freestone, population 32, Wild Flour's wood-fired brick oven turns out breads so wonderfully crunchy-crusty that they have a cult following. Some 900 loaves in a variety of flavors are pulled from the oven each day. On the chalkboard menu, in addition to loaves of the day, you'll find whipping cream scones both sweet and savory (some gluten-free) and fougasse redolent of cheese and herbs. And, oh, those gigantic cinnamon, walnut, and raisin sticky buns! Specialty coffee drinks are also available.

If you can't wait to bite in, wander out to the back garden that supplies the fresh fruit, herbs, and vegetables baked into the breads. The baking goes on Friday through Monday throughout the year including holidays, save for Christmas Day.

140 Bohemian Hwy., Freestone 95472
(707) 874-2938, wildflourbread.com

BE A HAPPY OUTSIDER
AT RAMEN GAIJIN

If you're in a pub mood Japanese style, snag one of the seats at the izakaya counter. Sip your sake, beer, wine, or craft cocktail and watch the goings-on in the kitchen while you wait for what you ordered—perhaps yakitori or a succulent Hokkaido scallop brushed with barrel-aged sake and chives. Japanese paintings and hanging lanterns set the scene, traditional yet hip.

Head for the dining room if it's the signature ramen you're after. You can't go wrong—everything on the menu showcases elegant broth, handmade noodles, and pristine ingredients. Gaijin is the Japanese term for "outside person." If they were in Japan, chefs Matthew Williams and Moishe Hahn-Schuman would definitely qualify. But from their foodie's dream of a noodle shop, who'd guess?

6948 Sebastopol Ave., Sebastopol 95472
(707) 827-3609, ramengaijin.com

RAISE A GLASS
TO WEST COUNTY'S APPLE HERITAGE AT ACE CIDER PUB

When Englishman Jeffrey House visited Sonoma County in the early 1990s, the apple orchards in the hills of West County reminded him of home. But no one was making hard cider! In 1993 Jeffrey, with his wife, Angela, by his side, began production. Today, with their three grown sons joining in, family-owned California Cider Company produces the nationally known ACE Cider brand.

True to the couple's roots, an authentic Brit-pub experience is offered in a space behind the production facility, complete with darts and musical entertainment—but only on Friday afternoons. "We started out opening daily," Jeffrey says, "but the pub got so busy, it was cutting into my work schedule!" Twelve ciders are on tap or bottled, including hard-to-find seasonals. Dogs and picnics are welcome in the outdoor seating area.

2064 Gravenstein Hwy. N, Sebastopol 95472
(707) 829-1101, acecider.com

TREAT YOURSELF
TO AN ELEGANT DINING EXPERIENCE AT MADRONA MANOR

A flair for the unexpected marks Michelin-starred chef Jesse Mallgren's ever-evolving seven-course tasting menu and à la carte offerings that emerge from the kitchen of the Victorian mansion nestled in the hills above Dry Creek Valley. For inspiration, he looks first to the estate's organic vegetable gardens, orchards, and greenhouse, with the goal that every menu item contains at least one "of-the-moment ingredient" grown on the estate.

Elegant dinners are served in five cozy, candlelit dining rooms. The less formal option is the menu of small plates served in the lounge. Reservations are a must for the dining rooms; none are accepted in the lounge. Before or after dining, meander up the hillside beyond the mansion to stroll through the gardens that inspired your meal.

1001 Westside Rd., Healdsburg 95448
(707) 433-4231, madronamanor.com

TIP
Gracious overnight stays are offered in the mansion and converted historic buildings on the grounds.

TIE ON AN APRON
FOR A ROVING COOKING CLASS
AT RELISH CULINARY ADVENTURES

Sonoma's bounty of food and wine, coupled with the county's diverse geographic charm, inspired Relish founder Donna del Rey to create a cooking school with no schoolhouse in 2003. Lessons in unique rural locations, under the tutelage of engaging and talented restaurant chefs, cookbook authors, caterers, food purveyors, and wine experts, became known as Culinary Adventures.

Five years later, Relish opened a teaching kitchen just off Healdsburg's historic plaza while continuing to offer roving cooking experiences. Either way, classes are small and hands-on, and you get to eat what you've cooked. Truly hands-on is the snout-to-tail pork butchering class: cut one up and carry it home.

14 Matheson St., Healdsburg 95448
(707) 431-9999, relishculinary.com

EMBARK ON A SPIRITED VODKA JOURNEY
AT HANSON OF SONOMA DISTILLERY

Guided tasting experiences take place at a table overlooking the pond in the Spirit Garden, or inside should the day be iffy. While most vodkas are made from fermented grains, Hanson's begin in an organic vineyard—grapes made into wine and then distilled. The infused flavors are also organic: cucumber, Meyer lemon, mandarin orange, and habanero. (Some like their vodka hot!)

Six different tasting experiences are offered at escalating price points: a basic sampling of the flavored line can be combined with a craft cocktail, a distillery tour, chocolates and truffles, or a martini and caviar. Or choose the distillery tour and complete tasting accompanied by a plate of local cheese and charcuterie. Organic grapes, fruits, and vegetables—Hanson's vodkas sound downright nutritious!

22985 Burndale Rd., Sonoma 95476
(707) 343-1805, hansonofsonoma.com

MORE DISTILLERIES TO VISIT

Alley 6 Craft Distillery
1401 Grove St., Suite D, Healdsburg 95448
(707) 484-3593, alley6.com

Prohibition Spirits
23570 Arnold Dr., Sonoma 95476
(707) 933-7507, prohibition-spirits.com

Sonoma Brothers Distilling
7759 Bell Rd., Windsor 95492
(707) 687-5149, sonomabrothersdistilling.com

Sonoma Coast Spirits
429 First St., Petaluma 94952
(707) 331-0718, sonomacoastspirits.com

Spirit Works Distillery
6790 McKinley St. #100, Sebastopol 95472
(707) 634-4793, spiritworksdistillery.com

Young & Yonder Spirits
449 Allan Ct., Healdsburg 95448
(707) 473-8077, youngandyonder.com

TUCK INTO CUCINA POVERA
AT DIAVOLA PIZZERIA & SALUMERIA

Dino Bugica, chef-owner of this devilishly good eatery, calls his cookery cucina povera "food of the poor." But poor you would happily be tucking into any of his wood-fired Neapolitan pizzas. Try his "simple" zucchini flower and buffalo mozzarella Margherita. The pizzas share menu space with authentic Italian pastas, such as linguine tossed with baby octopus, bone marrow, zucchini, and bottarga.

Bugica spent more than 10 years in Italy learning the art of cucina povera, the time-honored tradition of making the most of whatever ingredients are at hand. The food is served up in a Geyserville landmark building done up with the chef's collection of saint statuaries, posters, boar tusks, and stacks of cookbooks.

21021 Geyserville Ave., Geyserville 95441
(707) 814-0111, diavolapizzeria.com

FOLLOW
THE ROLLING HILLS WEST
OF PETALUMA TO MCEVOY RANCH

Less than 15 minutes from downtown Petaluma, watch for the McEvoy Ranch sign by the side of the road. Turn via a winding, single-lane driveway into the stunningly idyllic estate created by Nan McEvoy, the *San Francisco Chronicle* heiress, philanthropist, and first woman chair of the governing board of the Smithsonian American Art Museum. Eighteen thousand olive trees—McEvoy is the largest producer of organic olive oil in the United States—and acres of grape varietals flourish in the county's newest American Viticultural Area (AVA), the ocean-air-cooled Petaluma Gap.

Seated olive oil and wine tastings take place in a pond-side setting of flowers and trees. Wine tastings can include a casual Mediterranean-style lunch; bread for dipping and estate-produced tapenades and marmalades accompany olive oil flights. With both, expect engaging ranch and McEvoy family-history tales.

5935 Red Hill Rd., Petaluma 94952
(707) 778-2307, mcevoyranch.com

TIP
Call ahead for a reservation and bring your walking/hiking shoes for the gentle Walkabout through the groves or the Hikeabout, an aerobic workout from the heart of the lower ranch into scenic ridges.

APPRECIATE AUTHENTICITY
AT EL MOLINO CENTRAL

Few Mexican restaurants make masa from scratch. Most reach into a bag of Maseca, powdered corn meal. Not so at El Molino Central, which earns its name by stone-grinding, in a molino, the long-soaked dried corn that becomes the dough for tortillas, sopes, gorditas, tamales, and many other typical dishes.

Time-tested authenticity shines throughout the menu at this unpretentious eatery. Order near the register, then walk past the kitchen and open the screen door to the picnic tables out back. While you wait for your food to arrive, be strong and don't fill up on stone-ground chips and salsa. You'll want to savor every morsel of the three-cheese chile relleno, shrimp tacos, chicken mole poblano tamales, or whatever you ordered that will soon be coming through the screen door.

11 Central Ave., Boyes Hot Springs 95476
(707) 939-1010, elmolinocentral.com

WAIT HAPPILY IN LINE
FOR CLAM CHOWDER
AT SPUD POINT CRAB CO.

Carol Anello mans the chowder pot at this seafood shack a step away from the marina, where the family's fishing boats bob in the tide. Although other choices are available—notably crab sandwiches, crab cakes, and an entire crab in its shell—it's Carol's clam chowder that places the roadside operation on the "must-stop" map for tourists and locals alike. Creamy and briny, generous with clams, and with just the right amount of potatoes, Carol's recipe is the all-time People's Choice winner in Bodega Bay's annual chowder contest.

So popular is the chowder that an addition was tacked onto the shack to accommodate Carol's simmering iron pot, allowing chowder orders to be ladled out ahead of other menu items. Even so, be patient—lines are always long.

1910 Westshore Rd., Bodega Bay 94923
(707) 875-9472, spudpointcrabco.com

YELL "YES"
TO AN ICE CREAM CONE
AT SCREAMIN' MIMI'S

"I scream. You scream. We all scream for ice cream!"—at Screamin' Mimi's, that is. Viewed from the street, the shop invites craving "ice cream now," its facade done up in strawberry trimmed with vanilla, with pistachio awnings shading the windows. Owner Maraline Olson made ice cream so good that her husband encouraged her to open a shop. In 1995, she scooped her first cone for sale, and the shop has been voted Sonoma County's best ice cream yearly ever since.

Ice creams and sorbets are made in small batches; seasonal, local ingredients are used whenever possible. "People wait all year for our lavender ice cream," Maraline says. Everything is made in-house—including hot fudge, caramel sauce, waffle cones, whipped cream, and cookie dough. As Maraline says, "We take ice cream seriously."

6902 Sebastopol Ave., Sebastopol 95472
(707) 823-5902, screaminmimisicecream.com

JOIN THE LINE
FOR PLINY THE YOUNGER
AT RUSSIAN RIVER BREWING COMPANY

Expect the line to stretch way down the block with a wait of three to nine hours when Pliny the Younger comes to town. Regarded as one of the best beers in the world, the uproariously popular triple India pale ale pushes the envelope with malt, hops, and alcohol. Brewed but once a year, it's released the first Friday in February, rain or shine, for a two-week run.

Once in the door, patrons are limited to three glasses over three hours. When the ale allocated for the day is poured, the brewpub's doors are closed. In 2020, 23,525 waited in line, coming from 14 countries and every state, adding $5.1 million to the county's coffers. After those two weeks in February, the rest of the brewpub's full line of ales and lagers take over. Most popular? Pliny the Elder.

725 Fourth St., Santa Rosa 95404
(707) 545-2337, russianriverbrewing.com

TIP
In 2020, Russian River Brewing Company opened a second location in Windsor with a one-acre, pet-friendly beer garden and two hours of free parking.

DON'T PASS UP THE JACKS
AT VELLA CHEESE CO.

Until Prohibition, a brewery held forth in a stone building located two blocks from Sonoma's historic square. With its closing, Gaetano "Tom" Vella saw opportunity—cheese. Cows were plentiful in the countryside, and a building was available. In 1931, Vella made his first cheese—a creamy, delicate Monterey Jack. Why "Monterey" and not "Sonoma"? Why "Jack" and not "Gaetano"? A novice cheesemaker, Vella patterned his first cheese on that of cheesemaker David Jacks in the town of Monterey. Dry Monterey Jack followed the soft; Vella's Italian neighbors wanted something they could grate over pasta.

The company is now in its third and fourth generation of Vellas, and cheddars and four Italian-style cheeses have joined the two Jacks. They are for sale in the small shop at the front of the building. All remain handmade in a process little changed since 1931.

315 Second St. E, Sonoma 95476
(800) 848-0505, vellacheese.com

SAVOR SALUMI
AT JOURNEYMAN MEAT CO.

Other meats, such as aged cuts of estate-raised beef and heritage pork, are displayed in the shop's cold case. Salumi, however, is the star.

When Edoardo Seghesio immigrated from Italy and planted his first vineyard in 1895, he brought with him a tradition of sausage-making. The tradition continued, with generations of Seghesios gathering with family and friends for wine-fueled sausage-making parties. In 2011, Seghesio Family Winery was sold. With that, Pete Seghesio, who had been CEO for 25 years, headed to Italy to hone his love of sausage-making with master producers of handcrafted, cured meat—salumi. Journeyman Meat Co. was born.

Grab a seat at an indoor or outdoor table and order from a short menu that includes sandwiches, pizzas, and an artisanal salumi board. Bites of cheese, olives, and perhaps pickled vegetables come with it. The perfect accompaniment? A glass of hearty red from a Seghesio vineyard.

404 Center St., Healdsburg 95448
(707) 395-6328, journeymanmeat.com

BECOME ACQUAINTED
WITH SMALL PLATES AND WINE
AT WILLI'S WINE BAR

In 2002, Mark and Terri Stark opened Willi's Wine Bar in an Old Redwood Highway roadhouse. Described by the Starks as "foie gras with flip-flops," the eatery introduced small plates paired with pours from an extensive wine list.

The restaurant was locally popular and acclaimed by critics, so its following was devastated when the 2017 wildfire that swept through the county took the roadhouse in its wake. Less than two years later, Willi's rose from the ashes with the friendly vibe and small-plate concept firmly in place in a neighborhood shopping center four miles from the old location. Willi's regulars are pleased to note that such favorites as Moroccan lamb chops, goat cheese fritters, and tuna tartare remain on the Surf, Earth, and Turf divided menu.

1415 Town and Country Dr., Santa Rosa 95404
(707) 526-3096, starkrestaurants.com

Willi's Wine Bar is the flagship in the
non-cookie-cutter restaurant empire the Starks
have developed through the years, all critically
acclaimed, all locally loved:

Bravas Bar de Tapas
420 Center St., Healdsburg 95448
(707) 433-7700

Grossman's Noshery & Bar
308 Wilson St., Santa Rosa 95401
(707) 595-7707

Monti's
714 Village Ct., Santa Rosa 95405
(707) 568-4404

Stark's Steak & Seafood
521 Adams St., Santa Rosa 95401
(707) 546-5100

Willi's Seafood & Raw Bar
403 Healdsburg Ave., Healdsburg 95448
(707) 433-9191

RETHINK DOUGHNUTS
AT CITY GARDEN
DOUGHNUTS & COFFEE

These doughnuts are so good! Don't even think of dunkin' them! Although coffee to go with is almost mandatory—order anything from City Garden's coffee menu, and you won't go wrong. Doughnuts are handcrafted, made daily from mostly local ingredients.

If you're pretending it's breakfast, choose the bacon maple brioche, glazed with maple syrup and topped with a slice of applewood-smoked bacon. The POG brioche—passion fruit, orange juice, and guava glaze—will have you dreaming of Hawaii. Rich and buttery cake doughnuts are crispy on the outside, with ever-changing glazes such as seasonal strawberry and dark chocolate sprinkled with three kinds of chocolate chips. From the "Old Fashioned Doughnuts" list, settle on organic Vermont maple syrup glaze. It's City Garden's best seller.

1200 Fourth St., Santa Rosa 95404
(707) 595-1932, citygardendoughnuts.com

ENJOY A HIGH-END DINING EXPERIENCE
AT FARMHOUSE INN

Reservations are a must at this Michelin-starred restaurant housed in an 1873 farmhouse surrounded by vineyards. Dine on an artful, ever-changing menu that depends on what's ready for harvesting at brother and sister owners Joe and Catherine Bartolomei's family ranch or discovered by chef Steve Litke on his daily farm stops en route to the kitchen.

One dish, however, can always be counted on: the signature "rabbit, rabbit, rabbit" appears as a confit leg, applewood-smoked bacon-wrapped loin, and small rack. An impressive wine list of mostly Sonoma wines promises perfect pairings. Locally crafted beers and ciders are also offered. Good news for designated drivers and other non-drinkers: juice pairings deliver all the taste while skipping the alcohol.

7871 River Rd., Forestville 95436
(707) 887-3300, farmhouseinn.com

TIP
The inn's 25 guest accommodations in the gardens surrounding the farmhouse promise a super-luxurious stay.

GIVE HIGH-TECH WINE TASTING A GO
AT REGION

Up to 50 exceptional wines from independent wineries too small to have tasting rooms are available for sipping at Region's cutting-edge tasting experience at the Barlow, Sebastopol's shopping, eating, and drinking marketplace. A wine-pour card is tied to your credit card, and off you go—one-stop wine tasting, self-serve style. Choose from a long wall of bottles displayed behind glass, stick your card in a slot, push a button, and have the pour you selected (one to five ounces) tapped into your glass.

A knowledgeable Region guide is on hand to offer help and winery information. Price depends on ounces and the winery chosen, with most five-ounce pours coming in at less than $15. Contemplate what button to push next while seated on the umbrella-shaded patio or perched at a table inside.

180 Morris St., Sebastopol 95472
(707) 329-6724, drinkyourregion.com

BE PREPARED
FOR AN ULTIMATE DINING EXPERIENCE AT SINGLETHREAD

Plan on spending at least four hours savoring the *kaiseki* parade of 11 Japanese-inspired dishes from chef Kyle Connaughton's kitchen, each a culinary and artistic masterpiece. "Exquisite" is how Michelin described SingleThread's dining experience when deeming it three-star worthy in 2019, upping the two stars awarded in 2018 a mere year after its opening.

Expect *omotenashi*, the "spirit of selfless hospitality that incorporates anticipating needs without having to be asked," from the minute you step in the door. No detail is overlooked—dishes appear on handcrafted ceramics, and lighting and soft music are engineered to subtly change as your meal progresses. Intrinsic to the culinary excellence is the restaurant's nearby five-acre farm tended by Kyle's wife, Katina, and her team of SingleThread gardeners.

131 North St., Healdsburg 95448
(707) 723-4646, singlethreadfarms.com

TIP
Continue to experience the spirit of omotenashi with an overnight stay in one of SingleThread's five guest rooms.

EAT YOUR WAY DOWN MAIN STREET
ON A GUERNEVILLE GOURMET TOUR

In 2009, chef-entrepreneur Crista Luedtke opened hip-and-happening, farm-to-table boon eat + drink, with its cozy dining room and umbrella-shaded tables set in a garden of perfect vegetables, herbs, and flowers. Next she established Big Bottom Market—a gourmet grab 'n go of sandwiches and salads, plus breakfast biscuits that are one of Oprah's Favorite Things. In 2014 she launched El Barrio, featuring tequila, mezcal, and bourbon cocktails as well as new takes on traditional Mexican food. And in 2019, she celebrated her heritage with Brot, a contemporary German *wursthaus und bierhalle* with quirky charm and classic Bavarian dishes such as potato pancakes and sauerbraten.

Unless you're equal to taking on Main Street in one overeating day, settle into Crista's first Guerneville venture, the chic and minimalistic boon hotel + spa.

boon eat + drink
16248 Main St., Guerneville 95446
(707) 869-0780, eatatboon.com

Big Bottom Market
16228 Main St., Guerneville 95446
(707) 604-7295, bigbottommarket.com

El Barrio
16230 Main St., Guerneville 95446
(707) 604-7601, elbarriobar.com

Brot
16218 Main St., Guerneville 95446
(707) 604-6102, brotguerneville.com

boon hotel + spa
14711 Armstrong Woods Rd., Guerneville 95446
(707) 869-2721, boonhotels.com

MUSIC AND ENTERTAINMENT

EXPECT STARS ON STAGE AND OVERHEAD
AT TRANSCENDENCE THEATRE COMPANY

Take your seat on a summer evening for a staging of Broadway's beloved musical classics at Jack London State Historic Park in the Valley of the Moon. The setting is both unusual and glorious: a ruined, roofless winery. The cast, all veteran Broadway and Hollywood performers, are knock-your-socks-off equal to the location. Since 2011, that has been so.

Pre-show dining, with musical entertainment, is bring-your-own picnics at tables in surroundings of a vineyard and meadow. Or choose your menu from the gourmet food trucks lined up in the parking lot. Sonoma County wines available? Of course.

1151 Broadway #201, 95476
(877) 424-1414, transcendencetheatre.org

JUMP ABOARD FOR A BUILT-TO-SCALE TRIP
ON SONOMA TRAINTOWN RAILROAD

All aboard since 1968, on what its founder describes as "a 10-acre, elaborate, table-top railroad that is outdoors and rideable." It is built precisely to one-quarter of the real thing and pulled by scale steam and diesel locomotives. Four miles of track travel through tunnels; over bridges; past waterfalls, ponds, and streams; and through the woods to a midway stop at the western town of Lakeview. A zoo of goats, chickens, ducks, llamas, sheep, and bunnies wait to be petted.

The whistle toots, and the ride continues back to the roundhouse, where four train-themed amusement rides add to the fun—the Iron Horse Carousel, TrainTown Airlines, High Iron Ferris Wheel, and Mine Train Rollercoaster.

20264 Broadway, 95476
(707) 938-3912, traintown.com

CATCH A PERFORMANCE
AT THE LUTHER BURBANK CENTER
FOR THE ARTS

"Enrich. Educate. Entertain." LBC lives up to its motto with bookings ranging from Women in Conversation—an informal gathering of remarkable women sharing their stories—to the gravity-defying Golden Dragon Acrobats. Jerry Seinfeld and Diana Krall have walked on stage, as has the Wellington International Ukulele Orchestra.

LBC has come a long way since its beginnings as a failing church purchased at auction by community leaders. (For several years, audience seating was pews!) Forty years later, LBC is a state-of-the-art venue with more than 230 performances annually in its principal 1,612-seat theater—pews long gone.

50 Mark W Springs Rd., Santa Rosa 95403
(707) 546-3600, lutherburbankcenter.org

OVERDOSE ON ACCORDIONS
AT THE COTATI ACCORDION FESTIVAL

For two days in August, Cotati goes accordion crazy. And it has for three decades. Thousands gather in La Plaza Park in the heart of this delightfully idiosyncratic small town. Squeezebox venues spill into adjacent streets, accommodating 40-plus bands and solo performers, from talented kids to Grammy Award winners. Bring your chairs and set up on the grass. Dance on wooden floors in tented stage areas, under the trees, and in the street to zydeco, tango tunes, waltzes, country two-step, and polkas.

Performers arrive from all over the globe—including Scotland, Italy, Lithuania, Germany, and Poland. Some show up in national garb, adding a costume-like component to the festivities. Accordions, accordions, and more accordions are heard from 9:30 in the morning 'til dusk. Proceeds benefit community causes.

La Plaza Park, Cotati 94931
(707) 644-0444, cotatifest.com

PLAY 36 HOLES
OF GOLF AND MORE
AT SCANDIA FAMILY FUN CENTER

Tee up your putter and send your ball through an opening and closing castle door. Send it uphill and through a chute, and find it positioned nowhere near the hole. Scandia doesn't make it slam-dunk easy on its two immaculately maintained 18-hole miniature golf courses. The play continues through windmills and past quaint cottages, ponds, streams, bridges, and fountains. As dusk approaches, colorful lighting comes on. Time-tested miniature golf became popular in the early 1900s and remains so today as something little kids through their elders can do.

But there is more than miniature golf to be had at Scandia: batting cages, both hardball and softball; the Lil' Indy Raceway; an arcade with more than 100 games; pirate-themed Blaster Boats; and a heart-pounding free fall from the Vertical Boom that ends with a smooth, slow, and safe return to earth.

5301 Redwood Dr., Rohnert Park 94928
(707) 584-1398, scandiafunland.com

HEAR THE HARMONIES
OF THE OCCIDENTAL
COMMUNITY CHOIR

In 1978, a group of holiday carolers gathered in the center of tiny Occidental and had such a good time that they didn't want to stop. Good news for you: they've been singing ever since. Two major concerts a year provide a unique musical experience—programs feature the personal, often quirky songs composed by choir members themselves. Lyrics are uplifting and often funny, encompassing a range of personal experiences. Harmonies are soulful, with accompaniment provided by community musicians on a variety of instruments. Through the years, Occidental Community Choir concerts have become "must attend" events, attracting far-flung audiences. As one choir member said, "It's not just the local yokels who love our vocals."

occidentalchoir.org

TAKE IN A BROADWAY-WORTHY SEASON
AT SRJC'S SUMMER REPERTORY THEATRE FESTIVAL

Months in advance, young actors and musicians apply to audition, and portfolios are submitted by would-be technicians, costume designers, and stage designers, all in the hope that they will be tapped for a summer of repertory plays and musicals at Santa Rosa Junior College. Most represent the crème de la crème of college theatrical arts departments across the country. So it has been since 1972, when two productions were mounted. Today, five rotate, with an audience of more than 25,000 applauding the performances.

In 2020, after a near two-year closure and $30 million spent, the campus's time-worn Burbank auditorium emerged as a state-of-the-art theatrical teaching facility, with SRT ready to take on such performances from years past as *Mama Mia!*, *Chorus Line*, *Sylvia*, *Hairspray*, and *West Side Story* into Broadway-worthy seasons for decades to come.

1501 Mendocino Ave., Santa Rosa 95401

(707) 527-4307, summerrep.com

LISTEN TO CLASSICS NEW AND OLD
WITH THE SANTA ROSA SYMPHONY

It began in 1928 when 35 local musicians gathered to present a concert at the Santa Rosa Elks Club. Today it is ranked among the oldest symphony orchestras in the western states, and nearly 100 musicians play a full season of seven concerts as the resident orchestra in the acoustically perfect, 1,400-seat, state-of-the-art Green Music Center concert hall on the Sonoma State University campus. Under the leadership and baton of Francesco Lecce-Chong, the fourth conductor in the symphony's 90-plus-year history, a composer-in-residence program commissions and premiers the chosen composer's first symphony as well as one of their shorter works. A series of Sunday-afternoon family concerts presents performances designed to awaken young minds to the joy and wonder of music.

1801 E Cotati Ave., Rohnert Park 94928
(707) 546-8742, srsymphony.org

BRING A PICNIC AND SIT ON THE LAWN
FOR AN AWESOME EVENING
AT GREEN MUSIC CENTER

The rear wall of the center's concert hall slides open, making for a unique summertime experience. No matter where you set up your folding chair on the terraced lawn, you'll hear and see perfectly, thanks to a superb speaker system and a huge video screen showing what's happening on the inside stage. The season kicks off July 4 with the annual Independence Day Spectacular, featuring a guest artist, the Santa Rosa Symphony, and fireworks as night begins to fill the sky. Shows continue through September with programming that promises something for everyone, from the Beach Boys to mariachi, from Johnny Depp to cellist Yo-Yo Ma. Comedy, pop, bluegrass, big names, and new talents keep the lawn and the interior packed.

Sonoma State University, 1801 E Cotati Ave., Rohnert Park 94928
(707) 664-4246, gmc.sonoma.edu

TIP
Pack an extra layer. The evening air can get chilly.

TAP THE BEAT
IN YOUR COWBOY BOOTS
AT TWIN OAKS ROADHOUSE

In the 1920s, travelers driving north on what is now Old Redwood Highway were happy to pull in for gas, a bite to eat, and something to quench their thirst at "the best tavern north of San Francisco." It was also known as a "rancher's bar," a vibe best translated as "Old West cowboy."

Today, live music is a passion, with bands playing almost every night of the week—country, but also honky-tonk, soul, blues, and rock. Take to the wooden floor for dancing. On weekends, weather permitting, the music moves to the beer garden. Fresh draft beers are on tap, along with a full-service bar. For eating, one does wonder what an Old West cowboy would have to say about a hamburger on a brioche bun! Even so, your cowboy hat and western boots keeping time to the music will feel right at home.

5745 Old Redwood Hwy., Penngrove 94951
(707) 795-5118, twinoaksroadhouse.com

TIP
Twin Oaks Roadhouse is the sister bar of HopMonk taverns in Sebastopol and Sonoma.

HEAD FOR A ROCKIN' TIME
AT SOMO CONCERTS

A powerhouse lineup (such as alt-rock band the Dirty Heads, Mexican norteño group Los Tigres del Norte, and blues legends Buddy Guy and Charlie Musselwhite) draws the crowds at the Grove, a solar-powered, 3,000-seat outdoor venue at the heart of SOMO Village, an environmentally friendly live-work-play community in Rohnert Park. Primo seating is for 200 on bleachers overlooking the 1,200-square-foot stage. Otherwise, bring your low-to-the-ground chair, find a spot in the Grove's redwood tree-surrounded courtyard, sit back, and enjoy a pop-up festival concert. Sound and lighting technology are excellent. Yes, food and drink are available. And parking, plenty of parking, is free.

1100 Valley House Dr., Rohnert Park 94928
(707) 302-8725, somoconcerts.com

DROP BY
FOR MUSIC AND MORE
AT JAMISON'S ROARING DONKEY

Throw darts, play pool, challenge a friend to shuffleboard. Add in a trivia night and a separate room for DJ and live music, dancing, and open mic nights—the Roaring Donkey has it all. A great cocktail menu includes 10 Moscow mules; Hibiscus Bliss and Peach Cobbler are favorites. A DIY Bloody Mary buffet is an every-Sunday-morning happening. On tap is an impressive selection of craft beers.

Despite its steel and reclaimed-lumber interior, the place has an Irish pub vibe. It is comfortably dark inside, as any good Irish bar should be, but a large street-side window opens the place to the outside world's passing parade. Roaring Donkey (or just plain "the Donkey," as it's affectionately called) can roar, but not so loud that conversation is impossible. Before you know it, it's closing time 2 a.m.

146 Kentucky St., Petaluma 94952
(707) 772-5478, roaring-donkey.com

RETURN TO THE INSTRUMENTAL PAST
AT THE VALLEY OF THE MOON
MUSIC FESTIVAL

When Beethoven and Mozart composed their masterpieces, their work was created for the instruments of their time. Enter Eric Zivian, pianist, and Tanya Tomkins, cellist, who came up with the idea of presenting Classical and Romantic period (1700–1805) chamber music on historically authentic instruments. In 2015, the first of an annual series of six summer concerts took place at the Hanna Boys Center auditorium in the Valley of the Moon.

Musicians and those with keen ears note that when taken back 200 years, the sound was more natural, delicate, and subtle than that heard today. Violins, violas, and cellos were strung with sheep intestines instead of nylon and metal, and the piano was a small all-wood pianoforte instead of a concert grand—historical and modern pros and cons to contemplate over a complimentary glass of après-concert Sonoma County wine.

(707) 509-3713
valleyofthemoonmusicfestival.org

ENJOY AND REFLECT ON AMERICAN-BORN JAZZ
AT THE HEALDSBURG JAZZ FESTIVAL

For 10 summer days, Healdsburg is jazz central, providing venues for real American-born jazz—"not," as the annual festival's founder Jessica Felix says, "watered-down pop versions of the genre." The festival is now entering its third decade, and performances feature internationally acclaimed musicians, leading locals, and talented newcomers on their way to fame.

Jazz is heard all over town. Attend concerts over dinner at restaurants; in art galleries, hotel lobbies, and auditoriums; and at free concerts in the plaza. Others are out of town at nearby wineries, where jazz meets wine-sipping in vineyard-edged outdoor settings.

Take note that Healdsburg's annual cornucopia of jazz has earned a national reputation for artistic excellence. Get your tickets early.

456 Moore Ln., Healdsburg 95448
(707) 433-4633, healdsburgjazz.org

SIP AND PICNIC
AT THE RODNEY STRONG
SUMMER CONCERT SERIES

Music and wine go on all summer long, June to September, on the Green, the winery's tree-shaded area set aside for summer concerts. Unfold your low chair and find a place on the lawn, or upgrade to a section of regular-height folding chairs closer to the stage. Come early and enjoy sweeping vineyard views of the Russian River Valley while picnicking from the basket you've brought along or one purchased from the assembled food trucks' tempting menus. For something to sip while picnicking and listening, Rodney Strong wines are available by the glass or bottle. Sit back and enjoy the top-notch talent the series has become known for since 1990. Among the recent performers are Melissa Etheridge, the Temptations, and Boz Scaggs.

11455 Old Redwood Hwy., Healdsburg 95448
(707) 431-1533, rodneystrong.com

MORE WINERY SUMMER CONCERTS

B. R. Cohn
15000 Sonoma Hwy.,
Glen Ellen 95442
(707) 938-4064, brcohn.com

Gundlach Bundschu
2000 Denmark St.,
Sonoma 95476
(707) 938-5277, gunbun.com

APPLAUD MUSICALS AND DRAMAS
AT THE 6TH STREET PLAYHOUSE

Enjoy an unhampered view of the stage no matter where you sit. That was a goal in 2005 when the 107-year-old Del Monte cannery warehouse in the Historic Old Railroad Square district opened as a cutting-edge, 185-seat theater capable of producing large-scale musicals—*Mame* was a sellout. Three years later, a 99-seat almost-wraparound theater was added, welcoming audiences to intimate performances, some with a sole actor, such as *Fully Committed*, and others a close encounter with a classic, such as *A Streetcar Named Desire*.

The Playhouse's roots, however, go far deeper than 2005. Live theater in the renovated warehouse resulted from the merging of two longtime companies, the oldest founded in 1972. With that, the 6th Street Playhouse claims nearly 50 years of treading the boards as Sonoma County's oldest operating community theater.

52 W Sixth St., Santa Rosa 95401
(707) 523-4185
6thstreetplayhouse.com

TIP
Parking on the lot is convenient, safe, and free.

MORE COMMUNITY THEATER

Cinnabar Theater
3333 Petaluma Blvd. N, Petaluma 94952
(707) 763-8920, cinnabartheater.org

Cloverdale Performing Arts Center
209 N Cloverdale Blvd., Cloverdale 95425
(707) 894-2214, cloverdaleperformingarts.com

Left Edge Theatre
50 Mark W Springs Rd., Santa Rosa 95403
(707) 546-3600, leftedgetheatre.com

Main Stage West
104 N Main St., Sebastopol 95472
(707) 823-0177, mainstagewest.com

Raven Performing Arts Theater
115 N St., Healdsburg 95448
(707) 433-6335, raventheater.org

Spreckels Performing Arts Center
5409 Snyder Ln., Rohnert Park 94928
(707) 588-3400, rpcity.org

The Imaginists
461 Sebastopol Ave., Santa Rosa 95401
(707) 528-7554, theimaginists.org

SPORTS AND RECREATION

TOUR THE "SONOMA'S SERENGETI" WILD BEAST ENCAMPMENT
AT SAFARI WEST

Rhinos, giraffes, ostriches, cheetahs, water buffalos, hyenas, and flamingos—some 1,000 animals representing 80 species of primates, carnivores, hoofed animals, birds, and reptiles are at home on 400 acres of trees, grasslands, and lakes in the oak-studded Mayacamas foothills. All can be viewed, safely and closely, from your seat in an open-air, 12-passenger touring vehicle.

Safari West owners Peter and Nancy Lang describe their now-super-popular venture as a slow build. "On our first day of opening in 1993, nobody came," Nancy recalls. Nevertheless, the Langs remained dedicated to a meaningful, informative, authentic experience. Today, Safari West is a "must see."

Extend your *Out of Africa* adventure with an overnight stay in one of 30 luxuriously appointed canvas-walled tent cabins—nocturnal calls and snorts included.

3115 Porter Creek Rd., Santa Rosa 95404
(800) 616-2695, safariwest.com

TAKE YOURSELF OUT
TO A SONOMA STOMPERS BALL GAME

The crack of bat hitting ball—that's summer! June through August, the Sonoma Stompers play as many as 40 hometown games at the town's Arnold Field. It's baseball big time, minor league. The throw of the first Stompers ball in 2014 marked the first professional team in a dozen years to call Sonoma County home. Since then, the team has made sports history: in 2015, the starting pitcher was the first openly gay player in baseball history; two female players joined the roster in 2016 as the first professional female battery; and in 2017, the team was the subject of *The Only Rule Is It Has to Work*, a *New York Times* best seller.

Impressive wins keep the stands at Arnold Field full. Diamond Level seats are primo, shaded, and cushioned with backs.

180 First St. W, Sonoma 95476
(707) 938-7277, stompersbaseball.com

LET THE GOOD TIMES ROLL
AT 7TEN SOCIAL

If you're good at multitasking, or just a mite bored at rolling a ball toward a set of pins at your usual spot, head for 7Ten Social at the Epicenter, a 130,000-square-foot warehouse turned fun, fitness, and food wonderland.

Bowling here is a head twirler. Overhead, colored LED lights turn the alleys psychedelic. A humongous 60-foot-long wall over the lanes showcases live sports—soccer, baseball, whatever—for watching while awaiting your turn with the ball. Music to bowl by is in the background. Everything from pizzas to chicken wings and salads to desserts can be ordered from the Victory House bar, situated directly behind the lanes. Your order is delivered to your comfy, alley-side seat, as are specialty cocktails, beer, and wine to sip as you contemplate all of the above along with your score.

3215 Coffey Ln., Santa Rosa 95403
(707) 757-9031, visitepicenter.com

WATCH FOR WHALES
AT BODEGA HEAD

Bundle up, bring your binoculars, and join the crowds hoping to catch sight of spouting whales as they pass through. Lucky you if you catch a fluke (tail) display as one dives in search of krill, the oily shrimp-like creatures found in abundance along the coastline. Bodega Head, a rocky headland jutting out to sea, is Sonoma County's number-one spot for whale watching. Prime watching is roughly January through mid-May, when some 20,000 gray whales, the most abundant species, pass by on their way to Alaska. On weekends, volunteers share information and spotting scopes. In fall it happens again as pods travel past Bodega Head on their way south to Baja's breeding and calving grounds. "Thar she blows!"

Southern end of 17-mile-long Sonoma Coast State Park

VIEW THE STARS AND WALK THE SOLAR SYSTEM
AT SUGARLOAF RIDGE STATE PARK

The dark night sky of Sugarloaf Ridge makes for perfect stargazing. On select weekends throughout the year, the park's Robert Ferguson Observatory, Northern California's most active public observatory, rolls back its peaked roofs for spectacular state-of-the-art night and solar viewing.

Come back in the daytime to take the four-and-a-half-mile scale-model Planet Walk. Signs along the way let you know where you are in the solar system. Every step moves you through a million miles of space; take one step every five seconds, and you'll be walking at the speed of light. Bring water and good walking shoes, and note that between Uranus and Neptune, the walking gets steep and rocky.

2605 Adobe Canyon Rd., Kenwood 95452
(707) 833-5712, parks.ca.gov

TIP

Sonoma County has 11 state parks and 50 regional parks providing hiking trails short and long, easy and demanding, from seaside to interior mountain peaks.

TEE UP
IN THE REDWOODS
AT NORTHWOOD GOLF CLUB

It's nine holes, but don't turn up your nose. You'll be teeing off on a course designed in 1929 by acclaimed Scottish golf course architect Alister Mackenzie—think Augusta National and Cypress Point among his world-class tracks. Mackenzie was called in so that members of the famous—or infamous, according to your point of view—San Francisco-based Bohemian Club could have a place to golf during their Russian River summer encampments at Bohemian Grove, which continue to this day. Mackenzie's play curls inside a loop of the river and meanders through a redwood forest. The challenge is to negotiate the tight fairways, grown tighter through the years as the trees have grown, without playing bumper golf off the gigantic trees.

19400 Hwy. 116, Monte Rio 95462
(707) 865-1116, northwoodgolf.com

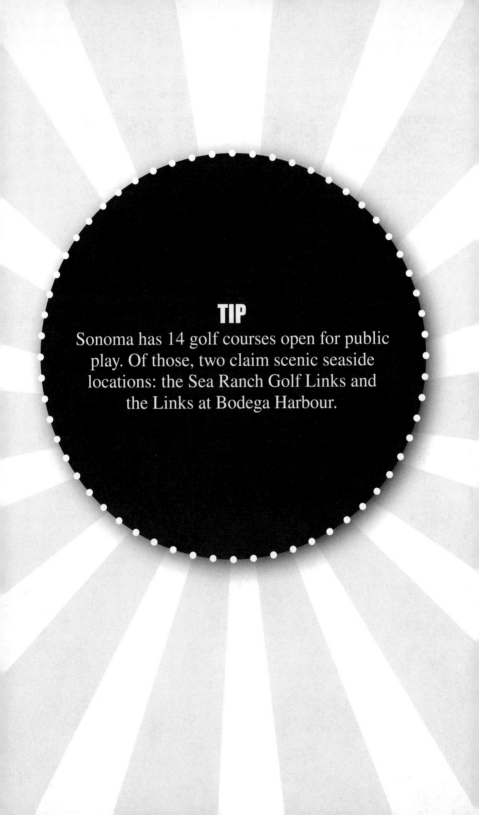

TIP

Sonoma has 14 golf courses open for public play. Of those, two claim scenic seaside locations: the Sea Ranch Golf Links and the Links at Bodega Harbour.

TAKE A PEACEFUL PADDLE
WITH RIVER'S EDGE
KAYAK & CANOE TRIPS

There are no rapids here, but enough bends and ripples to add just the right smidgen of adventure to your five- or 15-mile paddle on the Upper Russian River. Check in with the outfitter at Healdsburg Memorial Bridge and hop a shuttle to your starting point. The beach staff gets you going, and off you float into clear water with nothing but scenery on either side. Expect to spy plenty of wildlife—turtles basking in the sun, ducks, osprey, herons, and river otters. Pull out at a sandy cove for a swim or a picnic, or both. Peaceful, quiet, relaxing. In three to five hours, depending on how much you dawdle, you'll be back at the Memorial Bridge. Thinking about making it a family outing? Great, if your kids are aged four plus.

1 Healdsburg Ave., Healdsburg 95448
(707) 433-7247, riversedgekayakandcanoe.com

TIP

Explore the lower portion of the
Russian River with Burke's Canoe Trips'
self-guided 10-mile excursions.

8600 River Rd., Forestville 95436

(707) 887-1222

burkescanoetrips.com

HAVE FUN IN THE SKY AND SAND
AT DORAN REGIONAL PARK

There's no better place to launch a kite than on this two-mile curve of wide beach that protects Bodega's tucked-in harbor from Bodega Bay. Winds can be counted upon, and there's plenty of flat sand to run on as you encourage your flyer to get up in the air. Park in the Doran Regional Park lot or, better yet, leave your car in the Bird Walk Coastal Access Trail lot along Highway 1. Enjoy a walk of a bit more than a mile that loops through a saltwater marsh and circles two freshwater ponds before crossing the pedestrian Cheney Creek Bridge to the beach—a bird-watcher's heaven all the way.

Need a kite? Colorful and quirky Candy & Kites in Bodega Bay stocks the largest selection of sport kites and single-line kites on the North Coast. As for the candy, saltwater taffy is a specialty.

Doran Regional Park
201 Doran Beach Rd.,
Bodega Bay 94923
(707) 875-3540

Candy & Kites
1415 Hwy. 1, Bodega Bay 94923
(707) 875-3777, candyandkites.com

TIP

Along with your kite, bring tools to build a sandcastle on the annual mid-May Castles & Kites Day. Gather sand-construction inspiration from amateur creations and those of expert beach sculptors.

CRANE YOUR NECK TO SEE TREETOPS
AT ARMSTRONG REDWOODS STATE NATURAL RESERVE

Hike among the world's oldest and tallest living things, some as high as a football field is long. A path will take you to one redwood estimated to be more than 1,400 years old, the most elderly in the grove. Try to get your arms around one of the giants from a hugging platform—you'll need several others with you, holding hands, to make it possible. Pause at a tree that's a mass of unusual and massive burl formations—burls can weigh up to a ton. Ironically, Armstrong Redwoods, one of Sonoma's few remaining stands of old-growth redwoods, was set aside in the 1870s by Colonel James Armstrong, a lumberman who amassed a fortune clear-cutting the forests. Trails through the 805-acre reserve are fairly short, but string them together and you'll have a varied hike of six or so miles.

17000 Armstrong Woods Rd., Guerneville 95446
(707) 869-9177

TIP
If you want more of a workout, take a trail into adjacent Austin Creek State Recreation Area, which has 20 miles of hiking paths.

SPEND A THEME-PARK DAY
AT FRANCIS FORD COPPOLA WINERY

Swim in two pools joined by a swim-under bridge with a pool café reminiscent of a beach bar. Rent a *cabine* for changing; lounge chairs invite sunbathing. Four bocce courts and tables for card and board games are on the lawn. Something is always scheduled in the pavilion, from danceable music to puppet shows. Bring the kids and grandparents, too—the theme, according to Coppola, is "Life. Life with a happy Italian feeling."

Inside, five decades of Coppola productions are displayed, including the automobile from *Tucker* rotating on a slow-moving disc. Interspersed is what Coppola calls "retail"—shelves filled with everything from a red espresso machine to his signature beret; for kids, there are wind-up birds that fly around and kits for crafts.

Stay for lunch or dinner; the restaurant has stunning views. For wine, one with a Director's Cut label would be an appropriate choice.

300 Via Archimedes, Geyserville 95441
(707) 857-1471, francisfordcoppolawinery.com

PLAY IN THE WATER AND ENJOY SCENIC BEAUTY
AT LAKE SONOMA

Recreational opportunities abound at this reservoir playland, with its 50 miles of sprawling shoreline enveloping 2,700 acres of water surrounded by nearly 18,000 acres of preserved land. Take your pick of water and land fun, Putter about the lake in your own boat or rent one at the marina. Try jet-boating or canoe paddling. Go water skiing, have a picnic, swim, and fish for large and smallmouth bass, catfish, sunfish, and—if you're lucky—rainbow trout. Camping options include setting up for the night at 100 boat-in sites, some enticingly remote. You can also go horseback riding and mountain biking; hike meandering shoreline trails or trek into remote and rugged redwood groves and oak woodlands. There's even archery and Frisbee golf! No wonder more than one million people make their way to Lake Sonoma each year.

3333 Skaggs Springs Rd., Geyserville 95441
(707) 431-4533
spn.usace.army.mil/Missions/Recreation/Lake-Sonoma

TIP
Visit the fish hatchery at the Visitor Center to watch spawning salmon and steelhead jump seven steps to reach the top of the fish ladder.

ZIP THROUGH THE REDWOODS
ON A SONOMA CANOPY TOUR

Soar among and over majestic redwoods on the Tree Tops Tour, the more heart-pounding of the two zipline flights at Sonoma Zipline Adventures. Zoom along at up to 40 miles per hour, 250 feet in the air, with seven zips and two sky bridges to cross on what adds up to a half-mile ride, with panoramic views all the way. The Forest Flight Tour is a bit lower and slower. Book the Forest Flight as a nighttime adventure and add in the moon and stars. For both the Tree Tops and Forest Flight tours, you'll climb a 30-foot spiral staircase to the starting platform to be harnessed and readied for takeoff. Fear not—informative, knowledgeable, entertaining guides will be with you throughout your flight's adrenalin-rush moments. At the end, a 60-foot rappel returns you to earth.

6250 Bohemian Hwy., Occidental 95465
(888) 494-7868, sonomacanopytours.com

BRING YOUR DOG ON A VINEYARD HIKE
AT KUNDE FAMILY WINERY

Put your four-legged friend on a leash and join fourth-generation winegrower Jeff Kunde and his wife, Roberta, along with their dogs, Cooper and Kalie, on a fairly strenuous hike through the 1,850-acre estate's vineyards. The approximately four-hour trek will take you and Fido from the Sonoma Valley floor through oak woodlands, grasslands, and of course grapevines 1,400 feet into the Mayacamas mountain range.

It's fun and casual, and along the way you'll learn about wine-making techniques from grape to glass. Wine tasting—water for Fido—and a wine country lunch is included in the outing. A portion of the fee is donated to Sonoma County programs for abandoned or neglected animals. No Fido? No worries. Kunde schedules sans-dog hikes along the same path.

9825 Sonoma Hwy., Kenwood 95452
(707) 833-5501, kunde.com

SELF-GUIDED VINEYARD WALKS

Pick up a map at the winery for routes
of no more than a mile.

Amista Vineyards
3320 Dry Creek Rd., Healdsburg 95448
(707) 431-9200, amistavineyards.com

Balletto Vineyards
5700 Occidental Rd., Santa Rosa 95401
(707) 568-2455, ballettovineyards.com

Francis Ford Coppola Winery
300 Via Archimedes, Geyserville 95441
(707) 857-1471, francisfordcoppolawinery.com

La Crema Estate
3575 Slusser Rd., Windsor 95492
(707) 525-6200, lacrema.com

Schug Carneros Estate Winery
602 Bonneau Rd., Sonoma 95476
(707) 939-9363, schugwinery.com

St. Francis Winery and Vineyards
100 Pythian Rd., Santa Rosa 95409
(888) 675-9463, stfranciswinery.com

WHIRL AROUND THE RINK
AT SNOOPY'S HOME ICE

Peanuts afficionados have been circling their way around cartoonist Charles M. Schulz's alpine-inspired ice rink since 1969. It's a busy place, so be sure to check the website if you're hankering to lace up your skates and go for a whirl—public skating takes its place along with figure skating, private ice time, and junior and adult hockey.

If your ice worthiness needs sprucing up or if you're a first-timer, the Coffee Club is a two-hour, adults-only session that includes skate rental, a lesson, and refreshments at the Warm Puppy Café. Parent & Puppy Practice is for those age 11 and under along with their grownups. (Beginners take note: Chairs are available to push around until you're feeling ice-worthy.) In the café, windows alongside the rink make for wonderful viewing of the goings-on. Don't fail to order a Peppermint Patty hot chocolate.

1667 W Steele Ln., Santa Rosa 95403
(707) 546-7147, snoopyshomeice.com

TIP
A table in Schulz's honor is reserved in the café where he daily came for breakfast (English muffin with grape jelly) and lunch (tuna salad sandwich). Look for memorabilia under the table's glass top.

JOIN THE LOCALS
FOR A MORNING WALK
AT SPRING LAKE REGIONAL PARK

It's an oh-so-Santa Rosa thing to do, walking the trails around 72-acre Spring Lake. Join the parade of moms, and often dads, pushing prams; kids on bicycles with training wheels and true cyclists; strolling elders; and fast-moving walkers and joggers. Ten miles of trails offer dirt and paved options.

Mornings are especially lovely—reflections in the lake, birdsong, paddling waterfowl (even several pairs of swans), and fishermen out for a catch. Begin at adjacent Howarth Park, with its own lake, Lake Ralphine, and your morning loop of two lakes will add up to about four miles in a setting that makes it hard to believe downtown Santa Rosa is but minutes away.

Spring Lake Regional Park	Howarth Park
393 Violetti Rd.,	630 Summerfield Rd.,
Santa Rosa 95409	Santa Rosa 95405

TIP
From Memorial Day to Labor Day, an inflatable water playground is set up in Spring Lake's three-acre swimming lagoon for those age six and older (yes, that means grownups, too). Bounce, climb, slide, and balance on floating play stations.

SADDLE UP
FOR A GUIDED TOUR THROUGH THE VINES WITH SONOMA VALLEY TRAIL RIDES

Ride through the grapevines that make Sonoma wine country famous on one of Michelle Rogers's 11 calm and gentle horses. Sammy, spirited but easy riding, likes to do tours with his best friend, Jack, a seasoned trail and arena horse. Small-framed Archie is perfect for petite riders—wranglers make sure you'll be matched with a steed that suits your size and ability. Choose a tour through the rolling hills of the Los Carneros wine appellation. Or clip-clop through the birthplace of California's viticulture. After your ride, you can opt for a picnic lunch and winery tasting.

(707) 343-5511
sonomavalleytrailrides.com

MORE SADDLE-UP OPPORTUNITIES

Chanslor Stables
Ocean views and wave canters
2660 Hwy. 1, Bodega Bay 94923
(707) 589-5040, chanslorstables.com

Horse N Around Trail Rides
Sand dunes and beach rides
18797 S. Hwy. 1, Bodega Bay 94923
(707) 875-3333, horsenaroundtrailrides.com

Ranch at Lake Sonoma
Wilderness experiences
100 Marina Rd., Lot A, Geyserville 95441
(707) 494-4449, theranchatlakesonoma.com

Rollin F Ranch
Scenic tour of private ranch
100 Sparkes Rd., Sebastopol 95472
(707) 480-0800, rollinfranch.com

Triple Creek Horse Outfit
Rides at Jack London State Historic Park
2400 London Ranch Rd., Glen Ellen 95442
(707) 887-8700, triplecreekhorseoutfit.com

TRY OUT THE TRACK
AT SONOMA RACEWAY

Monster-energy NASCAR and NHRA drag racing bring as many as 100,000 spectators to this grassland- and vineyard-edged raceway. Between such fan-fueled events, however, the famed raceway stands far from idle. School programs, safe-driving programs, and performance driving and testing go on nonstop, giving you the opportunity of a lifetime to experience firsthand the famous track.

A range of possibilities exist. Pushing the adrenaline pedal, the three-day racing school will see you lapping the track in a high-performance car. Or, after one day of learning and practicing proper steering, skid control, emergency braking, and accident-avoidance techniques, you'll end up feeling safer behind the wheel of your own car. Your teachers? Those who know best how to handle vehicles: current racing drivers.

29355 Arnold Dr., Sonoma 95476
(800) 870-RACE (7223), sonomaraceway.com

TRAVEL AT THE WHIM OF THE WIND
WITH UP & AWAY BALLOONING

Float over vineyards and wineries, the twists and turns of the Russian River, and barns and grand chateaus. And if wind and atmospheric conditions are in agreement, perhaps take a look over the mountains into neighboring Napa Valley or view San Francisco 60 miles distant.

Be willing to get up at the crack of dawn to meet the pilot of your hot-air adventure—balloons lift off in the early morning when winds are most favorably calm for drifting. Coffee and scones await. Burner started, your balloon inflated, you'll climb in with a maximum of 16 others. Up and away you go, with your pilot doubling as able tour guide to the sights below. Back on earth, it's breakfast and recap-adventure time at a local eatery.

2200 Airport Rd., Santa Rosa 95403
(707) 836-0171, up-away.com

PEDAL YOUR WAY
THROUGH THE COUNTRYSIDE
WITH GETAWAY ADVENTURES

Meet midmorning to be outfitted and become familiar with the efficient cross trail bike you'll be riding 10 to 15 miles (comfortable gel seats an option, e-bikes available). With a professional guide leading the way, pedal off on quiet side roads, rails to trails, and designated paths, with four different Sonoma County tours offered. The Russian River Bike and Wine Tasting Tour mixes up great scenery with West County winery stops. For those who would rather sample beer, the Bike and Brewery Tour follows a similar route. Or choose to ride through the idyllic Alexander and Dry Creek valleys on the Healdsburg Bike and Wine itinerary. Cyclists looking to break a sweat should book Velo 'n Vino Bike, a 35-mile ride from Healdsburg to Asti and back again. Whatever tour you choose, expect a lavish wine-country picnic lunch midway.

61 Front St., Healdsburg 95448
(800) 499-2453, getawayadventures.com

TIP
Cycling can be combined with kayaking on the Russian River.

WALK WHERE MAMMOTHS ONCE ROAMED
ON THE SEASIDE KORTUM TRAIL

Pull into the Shell Beach parking lot and walk north on the Kortum Trail, named for Bill Kortum, a tireless champion of environmental protection and public access. Basically flat, with one short huff and puff, it's a trail anyone can follow. Boardwalks cover the wetlands, and the rest is well-worn paths. Stop along the way to take in endless ocean views.

Fifteen thousand years ago, when sea levels were dramatically lower, the bluff-top grasslands you're walking stretched miles out into what is now sea—a great prairie, a "Serengeti" of migrating herds. Look closely at the giant rock sentinel midway on the trail and note the smooth patches where passing mammoths rubbed against them, just as elephants groom themselves today.

Make Goat Rock your destination, then turn around and retrace your steps for a spectacular four-mile walk.

Mile Marker 16.8, Hwy. 1

CATCH YOUR OWN SEAFOOD DINNER
ON A CHARTER OUT OF BODEGA BAY

Venture out of the calm bay into the waves of the Pacific on the deck of a boat captained by someone who loves the sea and knows where the fish are. Come back with what you've pulled from the depths, hook, line, and sinker—rockfish, lingcod, salmon, halibut, tuna, and perhaps a giant squid or a trap of Dungeness crab.

Everything is included, from gear to safety equipment. A California fishing license is the exception—you'll need one if you're over 16. Dress warmly and bring binoculars for birdwatching and to spot whales in the migratory season. For landlubbers, anti-seasickness pills are a good idea.

CHOOSE YOUR CHARTER

Bodega Bay Sport Fishing Center
1410B Bay Flat Rd., Bodega Bay 94923
(707) 875-3344, bodegabaysportfishing.com

Miss Anita Fishing Charters
1500 Bay Flat Rd., Bodega Bay 94923
(707) 875-3474, missanitafishingcharters.com

Miss Vic Sport Fishing
1500 Bay Flat Rd., Bodega Bay 94923
(707) 888-8092, missvicsportfishing.com

North Bay Charters
1500 Bay Flat Rd., Bodega Bay 94923
(707) 337-0608, northbaycharters.com

Reel Magic Sport Fishing Charters
1501 Eastshore Rd., Bodega Bay 94923
(707) 875-2628, reelmagicsportfishingcharters.com

SVA Marine Charters
1500 Bay Flat Rd., Bodega Bay 94923
(707) 971-0847, svamarinecharters.com

GRAB YOUR BINOCULARS AND HIT THE TRAIL
AT SHOLLENBERGER PARK

Share the path through wetlands and marshes with joggers, cyclers, dog walkers, and, yes, avid birdwatchers who consider the park "catnip" for resident birds and flocks stopping by. It's an oh-so-Petaluma thing to do.

Once a 165-acre ranch along the Petaluma River, the land was bought in 1970 by the city to serve as a dumping ground for silt dredged to keep the river navigable. Gradually nature had its way, turning the land into a wildlife-rich habitat. In 1995 it turned city park, was named for a retired Parks & Recreation director, and quickly became "catnip" for Petalumans out to enjoy nature's serenity minutes away from downtown. Benches along the path invite taking time to enjoy wetland, marsh, and distant pastoral views—and the Petaluma passing parade.

1400 Cader Ln., Petaluma 94954
(707) 778-4303

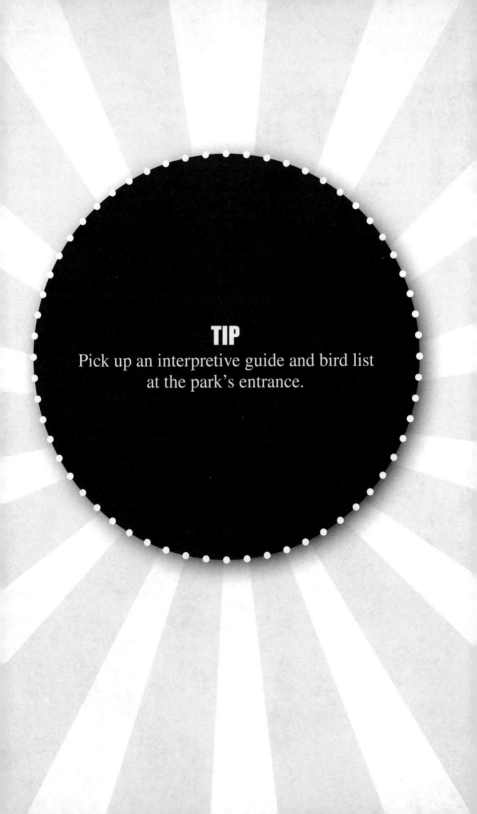

TIP

Pick up an interpretive guide and bird list
at the park's entrance.

Photo courtesy of Sonoma County Tourism.

CULTURE AND HISTORY

VISIT 21 CALIFORNIA MISSIONS IN ONE DAY
AT CLINE FAMILY CELLARS

Between 1769 and 1823, Franciscan friars under Spanish orders built a string of 21 missions south to north, from San Diego to the town of Sonoma. Each was spaced a day's horseback ride apart.

In 1939 all 21 missions could be visited, no horse required, at the World's Fair held on Treasure Island in San Francisco Bay—albeit in meticulously crafted, built-to-scale miniature. You can view those replicas today at Cline Family Cellars in the Sonoma Valley. In 1998, the Clines heard that the World's Fair missions were up for piece-by-piece auction. They bought the whole shebang and constructed a building on the winery property to showcase the collection. There's no charge, but consider stopping by the tasting room to sample wines from the Cline portfolio.

24737 Arnold Dr., Sonoma 95476
(800) 546-2070, clinecellars.com

TIP
Visit the northernmost and last mission built, San Francisco Solano, now part of the State Historic Park in the town of Sonoma.

TOUR THE DOWNTOWN
OF THE "EGG CAPITAL OF THE WORLD" AND BE AMAZED

Known as the World's Egg Basket for its booming chicken and egg industry in the early 20th century, Petaluma miraculously escaped the destruction of the great 1906 earthquake, leaving intact elegant Victorian-era neighborhoods and a downtown lined with iron-fronted architectural gems. On Saturday mornings, join a downtown stroll led by costumed docents leaving from the Historical Library and Museum, or pick up a self-guided map from Petaluma's visitors center. Self-guided maps also take you through areas of elegant Victorian-era homes and sites used in films, among them *Peggy Sue Got Married*, *American Graffiti*, and *Basic Instinct*. Hollywood has had a long-running love affair with the all-American appearance of Sonoma County's second-largest city.

Petaluma Visitors Center
210 Lakeville St., Petaluma 94952
(707) 769-0429, visitpetaluma.com

Petaluma Historical Library
and Museum
20 Fourth St., Petaluma 94952
(707) 778-4398,
petalumamuseum.com

LOOK
FOR THE PARTHENON
AT IMAGERY ESTATE WINERY

Sniff, swirl, and sip while taking in a gallery of work created by notable contemporary artists—think Robert Arneson, Shoichi Ida, and Judy Pfaff. Some were personally tapped, while others were chosen from steadily arriving portfolios. Artists are guaranteed freedom of expression, along with the assurance that what they produce will end up pasted on a bottle of wine.

Imagery's happy vino and visual marriage began about 20 years ago and now consists of nearly 500 pieces, with some 60 on rotating view. Sharp-eyed perusers will notice a common thread: the Parthenon. Artists are required to somehow, somewhere incorporate the Parthenon into their work, adding *Where's Waldo?* fun to the viewing. Why? It's a long story—one the person behind the tasting room bar will undoubtedly know.

14335 Sonoma Hwy., Glen Ellen 95442
(877) 550-4278, imagerywinery.com

TIP
Gallery Day artist appearances, label signings, and wine tastings take place on the third Sunday of each month, from May to October, from 1 to 3 p.m.

CONSIDER
THE FALLEN GIANTS
IN THE PETRIFIED FOREST

Wander two half-mile loop trails on a self-guided walk into a collection of the largest petrified trees in the world. Giant redwoods, felled by an eruption of Mount Saint Helena, lay preserved in volcanic ash for 3.4 million years. In 1870, homesteader Charles Evans was raking his pasture when he uncovered a log hard as stone. Evans, who became known as "Petrified Charlie," spread the word about his curious find. Scientists began to visit the site.

As you walk paths through the forest, you'll notice that many of the trees are nicknamed. Among them, the Queen was already 2,000 years old when downed; the Monarch, with a diameter of six feet, once soared 105 feet into the sky. On the Meadow Trail, take time to view seven-mile-distant Mount Saint Helena looking benignly innocent of the havoc it caused.

4100 Petrified Forest Rd., Calistoga 94515
(707) 942-6667, petrifiedforest.org

TIP
Although the Petrified Forest has a Napa County address,
its location is just over the border in Sonoma.

STROLL THROUGH AN OUTDOOR GALLERY
AT PARADISE RIDGE
SCULPTURE GROVE

Sculptures by Northern California artists stand among gnarled oaks in the hilltop four-acre glen overlooking the winery's vineyards and the valley below. Placement here and there among mossy stones and grassy clearings creates a sense of discovery as you come upon the sculptures one by one. Changed biannually, the exhibit's recent theme is "Resilience"—Paradise Ridge's events center was among the some 5,000 structures lost in the 2017 wildfire that swept through the area. An example of the theme is the work of Nick Taylor, who created two pieces, *Cosmo* and *Buster*, from petroleum tanks discarded after the fire. One well-known sculpture, not in the grove but on the property since 2013, spells out LOVE in massive metal letters. This is especially appropriate because the rebuilt building with its terraces and gardens is once again a popular wedding venue.

4545 Thomas Lake Harris Dr., Santa Rosa 95403
(707) 528-9463, prwinery.com

RETURN
TO *CALIFORNIO* MEXICO
AT PETALUMA ADOBE
STATE HISTORIC PARK

Locals refer to the park's centerpiece as the "old adobe." Mariano Guadalupe Vallejo, who ordered the two-story adobe and timber structure to be built in 1834, called it "the fort." So it could be. Built around a courtyard, it was so large that all aspects of Vallejo's Rancho Petaluma, the biggest and most prosperous estate during California's Mexican period, were overseen from areas inside the structure. On his 67,000 land-grant acres, Vallejo ran cattle, operated a lucrative hides and tallow business, raised sheep, and bred horses.

Informational guided and self-guided tours bring the rancho's heyday to life. Take time to become acquainted with the 41 acres surrounding the old adobe. The site is on both the California and National Registers of Historic Places.

3325 Adobe Rd., Petaluma 94954
(707) 762-4871, petalumaadobe.com

TIP
Visit General Vallejo's home, a wood-frame gothic Victorian in the town of Sonoma that he founded. It's one of six sites in the Sonoma State Historic Park.

BECOME A FAN OF FANS
AT THE HAND FAN MUSEUM

If you're thinking a fan is only good for creating a little breeze on a hot summer day, a visit to this jewel-box museum facing Healdsburg's central plaza will enlarge your thinking. Hand fans—some of simple paper, others ornately embellished—are showcased as a vehicle for understanding what the world was wearing, drinking, eating, and doing at the time the fan was held by its owner. While fans as a means of flirting is generally known, they've been used in surprising ways—as a formidable battle weapon; to drive insects away from consecrated bread and wine during religious ceremonies; and with pencil attached, to record who has the next dance. As founder Pamela Sher says, "Art, culture, geography, and history—it's all there in the palm of your hand."

309 Healdsburg Ave., Healdsburg 95448
(707) 431-2500, thehandfanmuseum.org

EXPERIENCE A ZEN IMMERSION
AT OSMOSIS DAY SPA SANCTUARY

Change into a *yukata* (cloth Japanese robe) and sip herbal tea while listening to calming music in a garden setting. Then slip off your yukata and settle in, buried to your chin in a fragrant cedar enzyme bath. It's a 20-minute escape from doing anything, pinned in shavings as the temperature nudges toward 120 degrees. You'll climb out happily limp from Osmosis's signature offering; it is the only spa nationwide to offer the Japanese rejuvenation heat treatment. From a menu of spa treatments, choose a massage in an outdoor pagoda amid whispering trees and birdsong. A creek-side path leads to a meditation garden built around a Zen Buddhist parable. Stay as long as you wish. It takes time to return to the non-Zen world.

209 Bohemian Hwy., Freestone 95472
(707) 823-8231, osmosis.com

OGLE LANDFILL-TO-LANDMARK ARTISTRY
ON SEBASTOPOL'S FLORENCE AVENUE

It would be just another quiet residential Sebastopol street of cottages, bungalows, and Victorians were it not for the parade of wacky sculptures amid the roses and zinnias in the front yards. There's the discombobulated waitress balancing breakfast plates and coffee pot. And a mermaid lying sideways on her multihued tail, not noticing that her scales are made from applesauce lids.

Each of the disarmingly cartoony sculptures is completely constructed from dump debris. Eggbeaters, oil drums, shock absorbers, watering cans, springs, hubcaps, and toaster ovens are all fuel for "junk sculptor" Patrick Amiot and his wife, Brigitte Laurent, who paints the creations. The couple live and work on Florence Avenue. You can't miss their house—it's the one with far more than just one whimsical piece on the front lawn.

patrickamiot.com

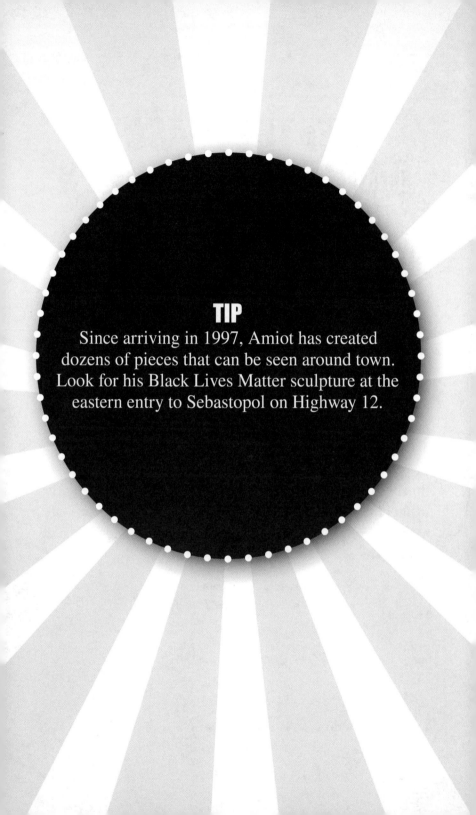

TIP

Since arriving in 1997, Amiot has created dozens of pieces that can be seen around town. Look for his Black Lives Matter sculpture at the eastern entry to Sebastopol on Highway 12.

MEET THE *PEANUTS* GANG AND EVERYONE'S FAVORITE BEAGLE
AT THE CHARLES M. SCHULZ MUSEUM

Of some 18,000 strips created by Charles M. ("Sparky") Schulz, about 7,000 are in this airy and happy museum's collection. In the "strip-rotation" gallery, changing exhibits of 70 to 80 original strips explore *Peanuts* themes: *Then Came the Dog* traced, via Snoopy, Schulz's lifelong love for dogs; *Mud Pies and Jelly Beans* drew on Patty and Violet's expertise as mud pie makers; and *The World According to Sally* took an in-depth look at Charlie Brown's little sister.

Upstairs you'll find a re-creation of Schulz's studio and a timeline of his life. Watch *Peanuts* specials and documentaries in the 100-seat theater. In the courtyard, look for the "kite-eating tree." Then walk a labyrinth shaped like Snoopy's head in the garden.

2301 Hardies Ln., Santa Rosa 95403
(707) 579-4452, schulzmuseum.org

WALK A
WILD ASIAN WOODLAND
AT QUARRYHILL BOTANICAL GARDEN

A steep, rocky, thicket-covered hillside cut with deep gullies that once supplied crushed rock for road-building has been gradually transformed into one of the largest botanical collections of Asian plants in the world. Forty years of annual foraging expeditions in search of seeds and bulbils from areas where they grow naturally in the wild created the collection.

Walk winding paths past water-lily-filled ponds, waterfalls, and glades of shade and sun where more than 10,000 shrubs, trees, and flowers from 2,000 species flourish in the informal abandon of an Asian forest. Then head for the Tibetan prayer flags at the top of the garden and linger to take in the extraordinary view of the valley below. Finally, make your way down through acreage that offers a reason to visit in any season, from the riot of spring's color to summer's lush green, through the brilliance of fall's foliage.

12841 Sonoma Hwy., Glen Ellen 95442
(707) 996-3166, quarryhillbg.org

EXPLORE A LARGE CHUNK OF CALIFORNIA HISTORY
AT FORT ROSS STATE HISTORIC PARK

The first stop at this 345-acre park on the Sonoma Coast is the visitors center. A documentary will fill you in on the Kashaya Pomo people's long presence in the area; the 30-year period (1812–1842) when the area was a Russian outpost supporting the seal and otter fur trade, for which the park is named; the Spanish and Mexican ranchos that claimed the land; and the American ranch held by the Call family for 100 years.

Primed for what's here, take to your walking shoes. Tour the buildings of the Russian compound and hike inland trails to the Russian-era orchard and cemetery. Visit the Calls' ranch house. Then follow the path to Sandy Cove for tide pooling. Binoculars in hand, walk the bluffs along a spectacular stretch of Pacific coastline watching for harbor seals, sea lions, and whales cruising in the distance.

19005 Coast Hwy. 1, Jenner 95450
(707) 847-3286, parks.ca.gov

TIP
Certified scuba divers can explore the wreck of the SS *Pomona* that sank more than 100 years ago and now rests deep in the water off Fort Ross Cove.

STUDY UP ON WINE
AT THE SONOMA COUNTY
WINE LIBRARY

This library within the Healdsburg Regional Library is considered one of the most comprehensive collections in the world. Some 5,000 books are archived, the oldest dating to 1514. Oral histories of Sonoma's wine families collected over the past 30 years are held in audio, digital, and print formats. Memorabilia, manuscripts, and old letters, along with vintage photos, posters, and wine labels, are beautifully represented.

Riffle through dozens of magazine subscriptions, or check out a wine-related murder mystery or a movie—*Sideways* remains the most popular. Locals plan their vacations, borrowing guidebooks to wine regions. Would-be sommeliers bone up for certification. Tasting room employees learn more about the wines they pour. According to curator Megan Jones, many others simply stumble across the Wine Library and are amazed.

139 Piper St., Healdsburg 95448
(707) 433-3772, sonomalibrary.org/locations/Sonoma-county-wine-library

ENTER THE WORLD OF *STAR WARS*
AT RANCHO OBI-WAN

Dedicated to "the adventures of characters a long time ago in a galaxy far, far away," Rancho Obi-Wan houses the largest *Star Wars* memorabilia collection in the world—certified in 2014 by *Guinness World Records*. What began in a converted chicken house on property owned by Steve Sansweet, a retired director of content management and fan relations advisor for Lucasfilm, has expanded into a 9,000-square-foot museum visited by fans and collectors from around the world.

Be prepared for an unusual museum visit. Rancho Obi-Wan is Sansweet's private, gated property. There are no walk-ins. All visits are docent-led tours of no more than 12 people and must be booked online. Plan ahead—the mostly Saturday tours are typically filled six to eight weeks out.

ranchoobiwan.org

RETURN TO A TIME
OF HORTICULTURAL INVENTION AT THE LUTHER BURBANK HOME & GARDENS

For 50 years, straddling the turn of the 19th century to the 20th, Luther Burbank's experimental gardens stopped passersby in their tracks. He was known as the "plant wizard," and today the famed horticulturist's creations continue to fascinate visitors. Peer into his Victorian greenhouse and walk garden paths where his varieties entered the botanical alphabet, from autilons to zauschnerias, and whirled America's farmers and gardeners into an agricultural age of plants tailored to fit. Docent-led tours of his modest dwelling are offered; Burbank's carriage house now serves as a museum and gift shop.

As you leave, view the gardens as most saw them when the plant wizard was in their midst—over the picket fence, marveling at the height of the hollyhocks and the abundance of roses. Still a showstopper.

204 Santa Rosa Ave., Santa Rosa 95404
(707) 524-5445, lutherburbank.org

TAKE OFF
ON A VIRTUAL FLIGHT
AT THE PACIFIC COAST AIR MUSEUM

More than 35 historic aircraft, most warbirds dating from the Korean War or later, are on up-close view at this three-acre field and hangar museum adjacent to the Sonoma County Airport. Crawl under the planes; look into wheel wells and bomb bays; and check out the cockpits of helicopters, drones, and fighter jets restored and maintained to their condition when in the sky.

To get the feel of what it was like to be the one at the controls, climb into the cockpit of the flight simulator. Choose your aircraft from a list of 15, from a Sopwith Camel to a DC-10, and pilot a 20-minute virtual-reality flight. Before leaving, don't miss the dioramas, models, photographs, and artifacts that tell the story of Sonoma County's participation in flight history.

1 Air Museum Way, Santa Rosa 95403
(707) 575-7900, pacificcoastairmuseum.org

EXPLORE THE PAST AND PRESENT
AT THE MUSEUM OF SONOMA COUNTY

In 1979, it was considered an impossible task: the inch-by-inch rolling of the city's 1,700-ton, architecturally significant 1910 post office two blocks from where it was slated for demolition. Today it is the heart of a museum dedicated to the county's past and present—a complex of two buildings, multiple galleries, and a sculpture garden. A collection of more than 18,000 objects documenting the region's history—paintings, clothing, tools, and photographs—is on rotating display in the mezzanine of the renovated building. Main-floor exhibits explore aspects of the past. Across the courtyard, a second building presents the work of noteworthy contemporary artists. Adjacent, the peaceful sculpture garden places large pieces in a landscape reminiscent of Sonoma County.

475 Seventh St., Santa Rosa 95401
(707) 579-1500, museumsc.org

FOLLOW THE FLOWERS
AT FERRARI-CARANO VINEYARDS AND WINERY

Bridges cross a tumbling stream and waterfalls flow into fish-filled ponds as you make your way through five acres of Italian-French parterre gardens at Ferrari-Carano Vineyards and Winery. Trees and shrubs are marked with identification tags, more than 2,000 in all; 25,000 flowering annuals are planted each year.

While the property is a treat to visit in any season, springtime is showtime at Ferrari-Carano, with throngs coming through the wrought-iron gates to "ooh" and "aah" over spectacular beds of tulips. Ten thousand bulbs are planted each year. With color blocks and hues thought out months in advance, repeating tulip peepers can count on a brand-new tulip extravaganza every spring. Opening date? That depends on Mother Nature. For a heads-up, the winery maintains a tulip hotline.

8761 Dry Creek Rd., Healdsburg 95448
(800) 831-0381, ferrari-carano.com

DISCOVER WHAT'S HAPPENING
UNDER THE SEA AT BODEGA MARINE LABORATORY

A small replica of a creature-filled tidepool greets you, along with a marine display of local fishes. If you were expecting an aquarium experience, that's it. Since the 1920s, the sprawling building overlooking the Pacific has housed laboratories devoted to the study of the 342-acre maritime nature preserve's diverse and abundant sea life. As an outpost of UC Davis, its research looks at climate change, invasive species, pollutants, and much more.

Time your visit for a Friday afternoon, when hour-long, docent-led tours are offered. Learn about projects involving sea urchins, crabs, sea slugs, and the reintroduction of purple abalone. After your visit, wander the laboratory's oceanside setting—seals sunbathe on the rocks below, and a migrating whale spouts in the distance—while contemplating what goes on under those white-frothed waves dashing against the shore.

2099 Westshore Rd., Bodega Bay 94923
(707) 875-2211, marinescience.ucdavis.edu

LISTEN TO VOICES PAST AND PRESENT
AT THE CALIFORNIA INDIAN MUSEUM AND CULTURAL CENTER

Stories unfold in the museum's two exhibit halls. *Ishi: A Story of Dignity, Hope, and Courage* recently filled one hall. Artifacts, interactive technology, storyboards, and photographs give an in-depth look at the man who emerged from the woods nearly 40 years after his Yahi tribe was considered obliterated. California Indian voices of today add poignant narrative to Ishi's tale of resilience and adaptation. In the second hall, *Precious Cargo* displayed exquisite examples of the cradle baskets women made to carry their babies. Included are small baskets in which little girls carried their dolls. Childbirth practices are also explored.

Don't miss the museum store filled with wares produced by California's first peoples; the store serves as a training ground for graduates of the Native Youth Employment Training Program.

5250 Aero Dr., Santa Rosa 95403
(707) 579-3004, cimcc.org

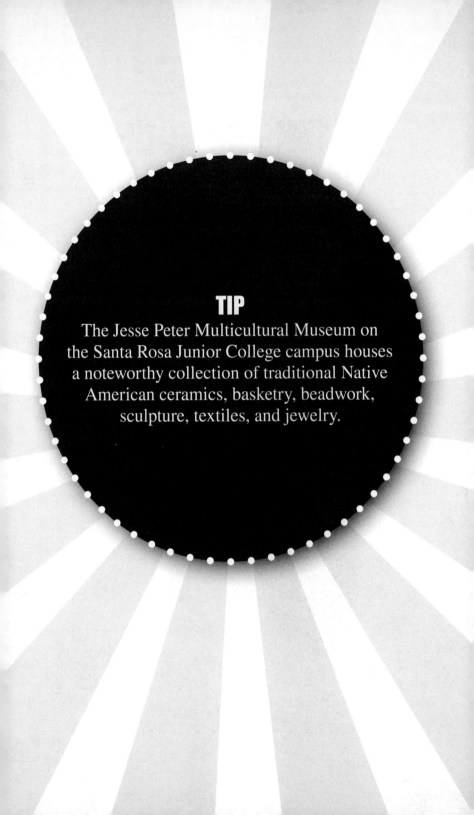

TIP

The Jesse Peter Multicultural Museum on the Santa Rosa Junior College campus houses a noteworthy collection of traditional Native American ceramics, basketry, beadwork, sculpture, textiles, and jewelry.

ENTER THE HOUSE OF HAPPY WALLS
AT JACK LONDON STATE HISTORIC PARK

The museum devoted to the life of Jack London emerged from a recent redo with a deeper and more intimate look at the writer's life. Interactive and audiovisual components bring unexpected aspects to the fore, such as his expertise as a photojournalist during the Russo-Japanese War. London's hardscrabble beginnings and his climb to writing fame are also explored. Other exhibits and artifacts tell of seafaring adventures shared with his wife, Charmian, and of his devotion to the success of Beauty Ranch.

With the museum's renovation, Charmian is given equal space. Following Jack's death, she designed and lived in the House of Happy Walls, its Arts and Crafts architecture a mini version of the couple's ill-fated Wolf House. Charmian is revealed as Jack's equal—independent, accomplished, and successful in her own right.

2400 London Ranch Rd., Glen Ellen 95442
(707) 938-5216, jacklondonpark.com

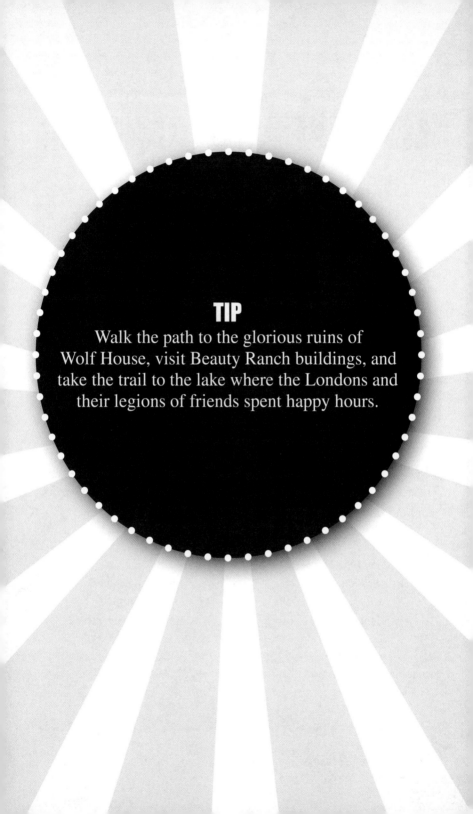

TIP

Walk the path to the glorious ruins of Wolf House, visit Beauty Ranch buildings, and take the trail to the lake where the Londons and their legions of friends spent happy hours.

LIVE LIKE A SEA RANCHER
AT THE SEA RANCH

The two-lane roller coaster (aka Highway 1) gets you there, echoing the county's northernmost rocky coves and wave-dashed cliffs. For many, it's a glorious introduction to a Sea Ranch stay. (Others unclutch their hands from the wheel, relieved that they've safely arrived!) Destination: a 10-mile stretch of land set aside in the 1960s as an environmentally and architecturally significant planned community. Its mantra: "to live lightly on the land."

Slanted roofs and unpainted, shed-like exteriors recede into grassy meadows, ocean bluffs, and hillside forests. Several original structures are listed on the National Register of Historic Places. Some 1,800 houses today make up the community. Many are second homes, creating weekend or longer rental opportunities. Become a renter, and all of Sea Ranch is yours to enjoy—tennis courts, swimming pools, and saunas, along with seaside and upland trails, sandy beaches, and tidepools to explore.

Sea Ranch Escape
35590 Verdant View,
Sea Ranch 95497
(707) 785-2426,
searanchescape.com

Sea Ranch Abalone Bay
36905 Green Cove Dr.,
Sea Ranch 95497
(707) 490-8291,
searanchabalonebay.com

STEP INTO A MASTER POTTER'S WORK AND LIFE
AT POND FARM

Monthly docent-led tours organized by the Stewards of the Coast and Redwoods gather at an unassuming archway marking the entrance to a clearing edged with redwoods on the banks of Bullfrog Pond. Here, Marguerite Wildenhain, internationally acclaimed 20th-century ceramist, worked and taught in the disciplined Bauhaus style—an aesthetic the Jewish potter mastered before fleeing Nazi Germany.

Pond Farm, rustic and peaceful, is centered by an 1870 horse barn turned teaching studio that appears ready for hands and clay. Peer through windows into the wood-shingle cottage, now in disrepair, where she lived frugally and simply. An equally simple, but repaired, guesthouse is now artist-in-residence housing. Wildenhain died in 1985 at age 88 at Pond Farm, listed since 2014 on the National Register of Historic Places.

17000 Armstrong Woods Rd., Guerneville 95446
(707) 869-9177, stewardscr.org

WALK PATHS THROUGH THE BIRTHPLACE
OF CALIFORNIA'S WINE INDUSTRY AT BARTHOLOMEW ESTATE

Hungarian count Agoston Haraszthy would be astounded at the goings-on at his rancho, Buena Vista, since he planted cuttings of European varietals 160 years ago. Kate Johnson, aka the "Cat Lady," built "The Castle" on the property, where she pampered some 300 felines. Later the estate served as a penal farm for "wayward women" and a hospital. Finally, it became a park owned by the nonprofit Frank H. Bartholomew Foundation, which is dedicated to the preservation of the property's deep winery and vinicultural roots.

Start at Haraszthy's Pompeian villa turned museum—don't miss the informational signboard in the parking area that includes a map. Be aware that the Memorial Trail packs a workout wallop in its three-mile loop of woodlands and stunning views. Vineyard paths invite a saunter that includes a pavilion on the site of the Castle.

1000 Vineyard Ln., 95476
(707) 509-0540, bartholomewestate.com

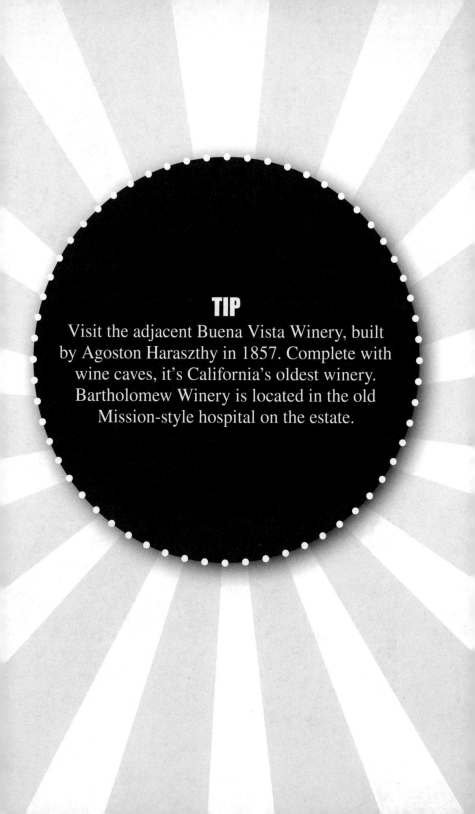

TIP

Visit the adjacent Buena Vista Winery, built by Agoston Haraszthy in 1857. Complete with wine caves, it's California's oldest winery. Bartholomew Winery is located in the old Mission-style hospital on the estate.

HISTORIC

DUNCANS MILLS

21 SHOPS
DINING

SHOPPING AND FASHION

PAMPER YOUR FEET
WITH BOOTS MADE FOR GAWKING AT THE APPLE COBBLER

Nope, the Apple Cobbler on Sebastopol's Main Street is not in the business of turning out the Gravenstein-inspired dessert. Inside the unpretentious shop, Michael Anthony Carnacchi, the "cobbler," creates handcrafted, custom Western-style boots.

Be prepared to open your wallet wide—prices start at $2,000 for basic calfskin and climb up to $7,500 depending on the materials and decoration. "Unfortunately," he says, "most cowboys can't afford my boots."

Precisely 372 steps, from initial measurements through final fitting, go into a Michael Anthony-brand boot. Each step takes time; don't expect your boots to be ready next Thursday. But they're worth the wait—at the final fitting, each pair comes with the guarantee that they are not only made for gawking but also super comfortable (ahem!) to boot.

227 N Main St., Sebastopol 95472
(707) 823-7204, michaelanthonybootmaker.com

PREPARE TO WALK OUT
WITH YOUR ARMS FULL
AT THE TOYWORKS

Jam-packed with time-tested games and toys, along with those excitingly new, Toyworks carries an astounding 15,000 items from 500 manufacturers. Thoughtfully arranged, fun, and educational things to do create surprises at every turn, making shopping for a gift fun for grownups, too! Everything meets owners Marilyn and John Goehring's criteria: items must be of the best quality, safe, nonviolent, and a good value.

So it has been since the Goehrings, former teachers, brought The Toyworks to Sonoma County nearly four decades ago. Play products cover kids age zero to 13-plus, from bathtub toys to physics experiments. Opportunities for dress-up are represented, from astronaut suits to tulle tutus. Personal service is a given. Free gift-wrapping, too!

6940 Sebastopol Ave., Sebastopol 95472
(707) 829-2003, sonomatoyworks.com

SHOP SUSTAINABLY
AT THE ANTIQUE SOCIETY

More than 125 dealers are represented at the Antique Society, making it more than likely that your treasure hunt through this vast, 20,000-square-foot shop will yield something yesteryear-stylish and sustainable for you to carry home. Art and cultural relics, jewelry, objects kitsch and retro, furniture, clothes and accessories, architectural salvage—it's all here, from those bird-shaped Bakelite napkin rings to that must-have redwood farm table.

Forget rummaging through dark and dusty shelves. Items are spaciously and thoughtfully organized throughout the light and airy building. Wheelchair shoppers can easily roll about; Fidos are welcome. Oh, and there's a bakery café, should a bit of sustenance be called for as you make your way through one of the largest collectives in the West.

2661 Gravenstein Hwy. S, Sebastopol 95472
(707) 829-1733, antiquesociety.com

TRIM SOME DOLLARS OFF YOUR WALLET
AT DUNCANS MILLS

Tucked between the meandering Russian River and the Pacific, Duncans Mills—a sawmill town established in the 1870s to supply lumber to a growing San Francisco—is today a hamlet (population 185) of a dozen or so unique shops.

Pig Alley offers an eclectic mix of things you didn't know you needed, such as ceramic handwarmer mugs. Antiquarian & Florabunda is an enchanting mix of antiques and flowers. Stop in at Christopher Queen Galleries and you'll find California paintings dating from the 1860s to 1940s. Worldly Goods offers pottery, jewelry, and clothing from around the globe. And Duncans Mills Tea Shop features loose-leaf teas, spices, and tea ware. Browse and shop your way through the charming hamlet, its Old West atmosphere firmly intact.

Located four miles from the Pacific on Hwy. 116

BECOME A DIFFERENT YOU
AT DISGUISE THE LIMIT

Whether you are off to a festival, headed to a theme party, or just have an urge to step away from your usual self for a day, Disguise the Limit has been costuming Sonoma County people for more than 35 years. There's a sales floor for those who are sure whom they want to be and want to keep what they've selected. The rental area is the place to browse if you'd like a tryout of a different you, or because Halloween is just around the corner. Have vintage-inspired gothic needs? Visit the Haunted Couture Room, where you'll find everything from corsets and lace to top hats and goggles. Try everything on in spooky dressing rooms that pay tribute to classic horror films.

129 Fourth St., Santa Rosa 95401
(707) 575-1477, disguisethelimitsr.com

COMBINE ONE-OF-A-KIND SHOPPING AND GARDEN WANDERING
AT CORNERSTONE

An elephant-sized red Adirondack chair marks the entrance to this small marketplace of unique shops. Eurasian Interiors offers framed artwork and antiques from Asia and Europe. At Potter Green & Co., birdbaths, firepits, water features, and chimes are just some of the items you'll find. Tesoro Flowers creates floral arrangements for every day and for special events. Fine fabrics and current designers are featured in the Loop's collection of sophisticated clothing and accessories. Sampling and bottles to carry home can be had at Medowcraft Wine and Prohibition Spirits' tasting rooms.

Behind the shops, a series of 10 gardens showcase designs from international and local landscape architects, along with five *Sunset* magazine gardens highlighting food and habitat.

23570 Arnold Dr., Sonoma 95476
(707) 933-3010, cornerstonesonoma.com

GET FASHIONABLY DRESSED IN YESTERYEAR
AT HOT COUTURE

What's hot at this shop is cold (without the "c")—vintage clothes, jewelry, and accessories for both men and women. Everything is at least 30 years old, with a focus on the 1950s to 1980s. Located on the same corner in Historic Railroad Square for as many years as the minimum age of what's for sale, everything you'll browse through is high end, in excellent condition, organized for easy shopping, fairly priced, and tagged with the decade of origin.

Should you have vintage pieces lurking in your closet, owner Marta Koehne would be pleased to take a look—pay is outright, not on consignment. With sustainability in the spotlight, Koehne views buying and selling quality vintage goods as reducing waste and offering workmanship and fashion that endure through the years.

101 Third St., Santa Rosa 95401
(707) 528-7247, hotcouturevintage.com

DECIDE ON AN ARTFUL HAIRCUT
AT THE GENTLEMEN'S BARBERSHOP

Make an appointment for a haircut and come out looking like a piece of art—elaborate art, incorporating color and 3D, swirls and geometric shapes. It is even possible to leave the shop with someone else's face on the back of your head. If Picasso were a barber, he would be proud.

But there is more than an edgy haircut to be had at this men's barbershop: old-school barber stuff, such as shaves that include a soap and brush lathering, a straight-edge razor, and a hot towel. And comb-overs that don't look like comb-overs. Step out of the chair feeling confident and stylish, as owner Marcos Flores feels all gentlemen should be.

9025 Old Redwood Hwy., Windsor 95492
(707) 838-8536, thegentlemensbarbershopwindsor.com

GO WINERY HOPPING AND SHOPPING
AT TASTING ROOM GIFT SHOPS

Some winery tasting rooms sell a few items, such as logo T-shirts, to remind you how much you enjoyed their wines. Others invite a spending spree with shelves filled with unexpected "must have" or "must give" items: CDs for listening while sipping, cookbooks, outfitted picnic baskets, exquisite silk scarves, Italian ceramic tableware, jars of local food products, necklaces and earrings, linen tablecloths and napkins, items of clothing (with and without logos)—and more, more, more.

SOME WINERY-HOPPING GIFT SHOPS TO GET YOU STARTED

Buena Vista Winery
18000 Old Winery Rd., Sonoma 95476
(800) 926-1266, buenavistawinery.com

Ferrari-Carano Vineyards and Winery
8761 Dry Creek Rd., Healdsburg 95448
(800) 831-0381, ferraricarano.com

Francis Ford Coppola Winery
300 Via Archimedes, Geyserville 95441
(707) 857-1471, francisfordcoppolawinery.com

Kendall-Jackson Wine Estate & Gardens
5007 Fulton Rd., Santa Rosa 95439
(866) 287-9818, kj.com

Matanzas Creek Winery
6097 Bennett Valley Rd., Santa Rosa 95404
(707) 528-6464, matanzascreek.com

McEvoy Ranch
5935 Red Hill Rd., Petaluma 94952
(707) 778-2307, mcevoyranch.com

Sebastiani Vineyards & Winery
389 Fourth St. E, Sonoma 95476
(707) 933-3200, sebastiani.com

Viansa Sonoma
25200 Arnold Dr., Sonoma 95476
(800) 995-4740, viansa.com

FEATHER YOUR NEST
AT SONOMA NESTING COMPANY

It was a gas station on the east gateway to town; today an array of colorful plants in varieties not found at a garden center fill the area where pumps once stood. That's just one of the surprises at this emporium of the unexpected.

Dedicated to making your house your own, the shop follows the mantra "re-use, re-invent, re-love." Shop an ever-changing showcase of ancient to mid-century collectibles, large and small; contemporary paintings; objets d'art, including exquisite pieces from Africa; and houseplants to enhance a room with life and greenery.

Mid-century furniture, hand-painted in unexpected hues, with just the right amount of undercoat and distress showing through, is a specialty. When time allows, the duo who owns the shop will consider dipping into their paint cans to turn that dreary piece of yours into a one-of-a-kind piece you will love.

16151 Main St., Guerneville 95446
(707) 869-3434, sonomanesting.com

CONSIDER SOMETHING FOR YOUR INDOOR LIFE
AT THE GARDENER

Outdoor furniture crafted from reclaimed wood, clay pots sourced from three continents, wrought-iron plant stands, and a garden guaranteed to make you green with envy—and you've yet to enter the renovated barn that is the Gardener store.

You'll find no shovels, rakes, or fertilizer here. Instead the spacious interior is filled with items curated by someone who understands that even the most avid gardener has a life indoors—someone like owner Alta Tingle, a former garden designer. You'll find handcrafted salad bowls, flower-fresh soaps and lotions, artwork for your walls, and a smattering of books that beg to be opened and read right now. And, yes, you will find some well-chosen gardening tools, such as the little scissors sized to groom something indoor and small, like your African daisy plant.

516 Dry Creek Rd., Healdsburg 95448
(707) 431-1063, thegardener.com/healdsburg

CHOOSE A CHAPEAU
AT THE HATTERY

Hat shops are usually hatbox sized; Jennifer Webley's brick-red Hattery is warehouse sized. Step into a hat shopper's wonderland—bowlers, top hats, traditional caps, cloches, sun hats, fedoras, berets, trilbies, and beautifully silly fascinators. Cowboy hats include Shady Bradys—think Julia Roberts in *Runaway Bride.*

Recently Webley bought the iconic Shady Brady line, necessitating a move from her small downtown shop to the current location, where Shady Bradys are manufactured in the back space. The front is for shopping. Try one on and buy as is, or have it made distinctively yours with a colored ribbon, a feather, or a flower. Completely bespoke hats are an option, too. Beloved hat grown shabby? The Hattery can restore it to good as new.

1240 Petaluma Hill Rd., Santa Rosa 95404
(707) 757-9971, thehattery.com

TIP

Don't miss the Hattery's collection
of vintage hats. Among them is a bowler
worn by Liberace.

BE THE BEST YOU
FROM YOUR UNDIES OUT
WITH STYLE BY MALIA

Who wouldn't want to be the best dressed and most approachable person in the room? Arrange for a consultation with Malia Anderson and it could be you, no matter what size or shape your body lives in.

Anderson, a fashion model, columnist for *Essence* magazine, and 20-year Sonoma County image consultant, provides a range of services, beginning with a closet audit aimed at creating new wardrobe opportunities from what you have hanging and stashed. A customized report includes style inspirations, color palettes, ideas for clothing suitable for the various parts of your life, and shopping and beauty suggestions. Then off you go, as Malia says, "dressed for the life, the job, and the love you want."

1007 W College Ave., Santa Rosa 95401
(707) 890-6005, stylebymalia.com

MEET OLD JAPAN
IN CONTEMPORARY COUTURE
AT YASUKO

Vintage Japanese textiles, including the sumptuous silk of old kimonos, are reimagined and recut into one-of-a-kind, timelessly elegant, sometimes edgy pieces of clothing created by Yasuko Bloom in her West County barn's studio loft. It's wearable art. Silk, her material of choice, comes naturally—not only have the Japanese recycled their silks for centuries, but her father was a kimono dealer. Truly ancient kimonos—national treasures—are never a candidate for her scissors. With kimonos in Japan no longer considered daily garb, her materials come from those tucked away for decades in Japanese homes. Most are from the 1970s onward, finding new life in stunningly contemporary blouses, vests, tunics, jackets, and dresses in Yasuko's Healdsburg boutique.

383 Healdsburg Ave., Healdsburg 95448
(707) 823-6157, yasukostore.com

SUPPORT LOCAL BOOKSELLERS
WITH A BOOK BUY
AT COPPERFIELD'S BOOKS

What began as a 725-square-foot storefront in downtown Sebastopol in 1981 has multiplied into four Sonoma County locations, with forays into neighboring Marin and Napa. While all follow the owners' original vision of a cozy, vibrant gathering place for booklovers, no two Copperfield's are alike: the Petaluma shop, the largest, has multiple floors. Upstairs you'll find a broad inventory of the latest and most noteworthy, along with magazines, cards, and a smattering of fun gifts, with one room devoted to children's books; downstairs is a treasure trove of antiquarian and out-of-print tomes. The Santa Rosa store boasts a café.

Each Copperfield's goes all out in supporting the community it serves, with something always going on—author events, book fairs, book clubs, and more. So it has been at bricks-and-mortar Copperfield's Books for more than 40 years.

COPPERFIELD'S BOOKS LOCATIONS

140 Kentucky St., Petaluma 94952
(707) 762-0563
copperfieldsbooks.com/petaluma

138 N Main St., Sebastopol 95472
(707) 823-2618
copperfieldsbooks.com/sebastopol

775 Village Ct., Santa Rosa 95405
(707) 578-8938
copperfieldsbooks.com/santa-rosa

104 Matheson St., Healdsburg 95448
(707) 433-9270
copperfieldsbooks.com/healdsburg

BUY *PEANUTS* CHARACTERS IN EVERY SIZE AND SHAPE
AT SNOOPY'S GALLERY & GIFT SHOP

Looking for a huggable Snoopy? You'll find him in a variety of garbs and sizes in the shop adjacent to Snoopy's Home Ice that stocks the largest selection of *Peanuts* merchandise in the world. Along with Snoopy, there are plush versions of the entire gang—Schroeder, Sally, Franklin, Lucy, and of course Charlie Brown. There are also *Peanuts* figurines, T-shirts, books, games, and CDs and DVDs. On it goes, adding up to more than 1,500 unique items. On the mezzanine level are displays of collectibles, such as numbered, full-color lithographs featuring the characters at their most memorable and lovable.

1665 W Steele Ln., Santa Rosa 95403
(707) 546-3385, snoopygift.com

EXPLORE THE BOUNTY OF THE COUNTY
AT A FARMERS MARKET

While grapes and wine tend to take center stage in visitors' minds, it's the county's agricultural abundance that creates memorable restaurant menus and fuels locals' kitchens. Farmers markets showcase it all. While fruits and vegetables abound in season, you'll also find honey and olive oil, eggs and cheese, wild fish and meats, fresh-baked goodies, seedlings and flowers, and artisan crafts. At some markets, music by homegrown talent plays in the background; others offer eating right now from food trucks standing by.

Twenty-one markets operate in 12 of the county's villages and towns, some year-round, others spring through fall or summer only. Rub elbows with chefs and chat with other shoppers and with those who grow or produce the array—it's an oh-so-Sonoma County thing to do.

farmtrails.org/farmers-markets

SUGGESTED
ITINERARIES

FAMILY FUN

• •

BY THE SEA

GARDEN VISITS

TAKE TO THE TRAILS

• •

FAMOUS FOLK

MICHELIN DINING

SPEND THE NIGHT

• •

WINERY VISITS

TO DO IN HEALDSBURG

• •

TO DO IN PETALUMA

TO DO IN SANTA ROSA

• •

TO DO IN SEBASTOPOL

● ●

TO DO IN SONOMA

INDEX

• •

• •

• •